YOUR FOREVER RETIREMENT

How to make your Nest Egg last forever

MEL CLARK

ONE

Live Forever?

_____

W hat's this "Live Forever' stuff? What kind of games are you playing Clark? Nobody lives forever.

Professional Financial Planners prepare their clients for retirements that will last until they are in their 90's.

Today, it's expected that at least one member of a healthy couple in their mid-sixty's will live to be 92.

The percentage of people who live past the century mark is steadily increasing.

There are reasons to believe consensus expectations are too low, too conservative. The first person to live 500 years may have already been born.

What if it's you?

"Life expectancy is the benchmark for what's typical. And it has been steadily rising. Were you living in England in 1850, you generally died in your mid-forties. That figure is four decades longer now. If you were

an American in 1900, you died around age forty-nine. It was seventy-six by 1997.

Not true anymore. Americans born in 2015 can expect to live to seventy-eight (it's a little more for women, a little less for men). If you've already made it to your sixty-fifth birthday, you can expect to live nearly twenty-four more years if female and nearly twenty-two more years if male. That's an astonishing 10 percent jump since the year 2000, and the numbers are expected to go even higher."

"Brain Rules for Aging Well" by John Medina

TWO

Who is this for?

_____

I f you have a working-class income. If you have the mindset, the strength of character, to spend less than you earn and save the rest, this book was written for you.

The wealthy don't need it.

There's an entire Financial Planning Industry (also known as Wealth Management) dedicated to helping rich people keep and grow their money.

Professional financial planning is labor intensive. It requires knowledge and skills and a lot of personal interaction. It's expensive.

The cost of financial planning leads Planners to specialize. They restrict their clients to those who can afford the service and for whom the service pays for itself.

Today, in 2019, even relatively new financial planners only accept clients with a **net worth** of more than $500,000. Or, clients who are young professionals with high six-figure salaries and the potential to soon reach that net worth of more than $500,000. These are also the people who generate the planners' high incomes.

Unless you're a member of this group, you're on your own.

There's plenty of information about money management available in books, courses, and on the Internet. Much of it is contradictory.

However, many popular financial planning gurus teach useful underlying principles.

The saving and investing parts are simple. Hard to do, but simple.

The more difficult questions have to do with why, how much, how long, and how to protect yourself in bad times.

This book is United States centric. The principles apply to people from all nations. But, the references to specific securities and legal constructs are drawn from my personal experience as a citizen of the United States.

Readers from other countries will have to research the legal constructs and securities available to themselves that are similar to the examples I provide.

I apologize for this inconvenience. There is simply no other way to deal with the issues.

THREE

What Is Your Purpose?

W hat motivates you to make the sacrifices necessary. What motivates you to spend less than you earn; to save increasing amounts of money every year and invest your savings.

Can you find contentment in living a slightly reduced lifestyle now in order to enjoy a significantly better lifestyle later?

The Marshmallow Experiment

"In the 1960s, a Stanford professor named Walter Mischel began conducting a series of important psychological studies.

During his experiments, Mischel and his team tested hundreds of children — most of them around the ages of 4 and 5 years old — and revealed what is now believed to be one of the most important characteristics for success in health, work, and life.

The researcher told the child that he was going to leave the room and that if the child did not eat the marshmallow while he was away, then they would be rewarded with a second marshmallow. However, if the child decided to eat the first one before the researcher came back, then they would not get a second marshmallow.

So the choice was simple: one treat right now or two treats later.

The researcher left the room for 15 minutes."

"The children who were willing to delay gratification and waited to receive the second marshmallow ended up having higher SAT scores, lower levels of substance abuse, lower likelihood of obesity, better responses to stress, better social skills as reported by their parents, and generally better scores in a range of other life measures.

The researchers followed each child for more than 40 years and over and over again, the group who waited patiently for the second marshmallow succeed in whatever capacity they were measuring. In other words, this series of experiments proved that the ability to delay gratification was critical for success in life."

Article by James Clear, https://jamesclear.com/delayed-gratification

Would you hold out for the full fifteen minutes?

In the words of Dave Ramsey, will you *"... live like no one else, so later, you can live like no one else?"*

Motivation - Purpose

If you don't know why, if your "why" isn't strong, it's unlikely you'll follow through.

Here's what motivates me.

I have many things I still want to do.

I want to write novels. I want to help people "live long and prosper". I want to teach Neko Ryu Goshin Jitsu in my own dojo and through books and video.

I want to travel with my wife all over Latin America and Europe. I want to spend enough time in each place to absorb the culture and the language.

I want to see my grandchildren grow into successful, independent adults.

I want to be a positive Christian influence in the world and in my church.

I want to "live long and prosper" and, if it works out, I want my wife and me to be among the first cohort to live more than 500 years.

I'm motivated to improve my physical health, my mental health, my spiritual health, and my financial health.

If you would join me on this journey, start by thinking long and hard about your purpose. Two good starting points are Rick Warren's book, "The Purpose Driven Life: What on Earth Am I Here For"; and "12 Rules for Life: An Antidote to Chaos", by Jordan B. Peterson.

These and other useful resources are found in the "Purpose" section of the "Recommended Reading" list at the end of this book.

Why do you want to do this? What will you do with the rest of your life? What would you do with Forever?

Really, what would you lose by trying? And, what might you lose if you don't?

FOUR

What Are the Risks?

S uppose you plan for a "normal" life span, meaning you plan to die sometime between 82 and 86.

You plan to "spend it all". You hope your last check will be written to the funeral home, and it will bounce.

If you die on time, you win. Your kids get nothing. But that's the plan. Congratulations!

If you die early, you win? Kind of? And your kids get some money after all.

If you live too long? You lose! Really?

You're alive but broke; except for what you get from the government. This is the default position of most working people.

No savings, or very little. Retired with only Social Security and Medicare.

For some, that's enough. If it's enough for you, stop reading and get on with your life.

On the other hand, if you'd like to *"live like no one else"* or if you want to protect yourself from unknowable but inevitable changes to Social Security and Medicare… let's think a little more.

A Personal Example

My parents were solid working-class people. Dad was fourteen years older than Mom and he was smart.

He researched Social Security and Medicare. He researched his company's pension and retiree health care benefits. He completely understood how Mom's financial situation would be affected by his death.

He organized their financial lives to take maximum advantage of the combination of benefits for which they were eligible.

When Dad died, Mom had enough money coming from Social Security and from his pension to maintain her modest working-class lifestyle. She was diabetic, but her Medicare supplement insurance from Dad's employer-based retiree benefit covered all of her medical needs.

Life was good.

But Dad didn't foresee Obama-care.

The "Affordable Care Act" (ACA) punished Dad's employer for the "Cadillac" health insurance provided to retirees. They dropped it.

In the end, Mom reused her needles for insulin injections and slowly went into debt paying for medication.

Dad's careful research and planning was for naught. Mom was left with standard Medicare and a standard Medicare supplement. She had the same "doughnut hole" prescription drug coverage problem as other seniors with chronic illnesses.

This is a recent, real-life example of changes you can expect in the Social Security and Medicare programs.

Congress modified these programs in every decade since they were created. It's impossible to predict what they'll look like in forty years.

You may want to have a "Plan B".

FIVE

Why Forever?

_____

E arlier you considered the possibility you might live longer than
expected. Longer than current average life expectancies.

Life expectancies increased a few months every year for many
decades. People got used to the slow steady improvement.

It's been pretty predictable.

Slow steady improvement might continue.

Today, however, there are a number of promising research tracks.
Tracks that might disrupt chronic disease and even aging itself.

Significant life extension could be possible in a few short years.
Maybe. Maybe not.

If it happens, I want to be able to take advantage of it. Do you?

Then there's the other side of the retirement equation. We've looked at
when retirement might end. But when will it begin?

My personal retirement is just around the corner. Besides death or the
apocalypse, not much can happen that will put my retirement far off
plan.

Many people are in a different situation.

A majority of working people retire before they want to. They or their loved ones get sick. They are unable to work anymore. Some lose their jobs and can't find another.

Instead of retiring at 66, as they planned, they find themselves retired at 62 or 58.

Because they apply for Social Security early, they end up with reduced benefits. They have less money saved than they planned. And, they are not yet eligible for Medicare.

Plus, instead of a twenty-five-year retirement, suddenly they must support themselves for thirty or thirty-five years; assuming no life extensions of course.

Whew! Talk about "headwinds".

Then there's the extreme. The FIRE community.

FIRE stands for Financial Independence, Retire Early. These are people who radically reduce their spending so they can radically increase their saving.

Most are able to retire in only ten to twenty years after beginning their FIRE journey. Some as young as 35 years old.

They're looking at fifty-year retirements and more, even without life extending technology.

A plan that would give you a 95% probability of not running out of money over thirty years may be wholly inadequate to support you for thirty-five years; forget sixty.

Sixty years might as well be forever!

SIX

What Are the Opportunities?

Living longer, perhaps a lot longer, is certainly an opportunity. "Yes", I hear you say, "but I don't want to be confined to a wheelchair with no memory for decades."

Me neither. But the promise of life extension research is to prolong life and health. Even now, many seventy-year-olds are as healthy as people were at fifty, just half a century ago.

You should expect the trend to continue, even accelerate. So, yes, it's a real opportunity.

What if you could also slowly improve your standard of living? That would be an opportunity.

What if you could ensure that, in the event of your early death, your partner could live well forever?

What if you could grow an inheritance for your children and grandchildren – even while you delay delivering it to them?

Would it be an opportunity if you could make a significant charitable contribution from your estate? How about if you could do it while you're still alive, without hurting your lifestyle?

Does it all sound like a pipe dream?

What if you could *"live like no one else, so later, you can live like no one else"*?

SEVEN

Proposing an Objective

To make these opportunities reality, we have to dispense with the standard Financial Planning notion of a "deaccumulation" phase of life, meaning "retirement".

You cannot support yourself forever if you're spending down the **balance** of your **Nest Egg**.

You can't maintain your lifestyle if your **Nest Egg** fails to keep up with inflation.

You won't protect yourself from changes in Social Security or Medicare without growing your Nest Egg faster than inflation. Nor will you improve your lifestyle over time.

And, all bets are off if you can't protect your Nest Egg from the worst ravages of the "Markets".

The implied objective is to grow your Nest Egg faster than the combined inflation rate plus your withdrawal rate. For the rest of this book, this combination will be called the "**base rate**".

Base Rate = Inflation Rate + Withdrawal Rate.

Inflation Rate is defined as the annual change in the **Consumer Price Index (CPI)**.

Withdrawal Rate is defined as the total sum of money withdrawn from your Nest Egg in one calendar year divided by the currency value of the Nest Egg at the end of the previous calendar year.

Restated, the objective is:

Grow your Nest Egg faster than the **Base Rate**.

To accomplish this, you must:

1. Precisely control your withdrawals
2. Manage market risk so you can "stay in the game"
3. Manage your investments so they grow faster than the **Base Rate** even while you manage the risk.

This sounds complicated, and it is. But, the financial tools available to you today make it easier than ever.

You don't have to be a financial superstar, a "market wizard", an MBA, or a CPA.

You do need to know some basic stuff.

You need to develop an action plan that includes a written process that you commit to using. And, you must follow your plan and your process.

The purpose of this book is to help you develop your plan and your process. And, to motivate you to execute them.

EIGHT

Structure of the Book

G oing forward, you'll look at each sub-objective in turn.

1. Managing Risk
2. Managing Investments
3. Managing Withdrawals

Then you'll tie them together.

1. Develop an Integrated Retirement Plan
2. Develop a Process
3. Execute
4. Definitions
5. Recommended Reading

You'll have noticed some words are in bold face type. The words in bold face are "financial jargon". They are defined in the "Definitions" section at the back of the book.

There are definitions for all words in the book shown in bold type except for the section headings.

Because some terms are used many times, they are bold faced only the first time they occur.

Okay. Time to start.

NINE

Managing Risk

"*How did you go bankrupt?*" "*Two ways. Gradually, then suddenly.*" This dialog from Ernest Hemingway's novel, "The Sun Also Rises", is a useful place to begin discussing risk.

The reference is to a character gradually spending his **assets**. First, he spends more than his income, consuming his savings. Then he spends everything he can borrow. Finally, he is out of money and no one will lend him more. Suddenly, he's bankrupt.

This is how a person uses up their retirement assets (Nest Egg).

They spend too much. They withdraw principle. The balance slowly shrinks. Suddenly, it's gone, but there's still life to be lived.

The dialog also points us to different ways a Nest Egg can be destroyed.

Gradually, by inflation or over-spending. Or suddenly from market risk, regulatory change, or a catastrophe.

- Ways Your Nest Egg Can Be Destroyed

1. Inflation
2. Hyperinflation
3. Over-Spending
4. Market Risk
5. Catastrophe

Inflation

In the Developed World, roughly the United States, Europe, Japan, South Korea, Canada, Australia, and New Zealand, plus a few others, inflation has seemed tame since the mid-1980s. People remember the inflation of 1973 through 1983 as though *"through a glass darkly"*. If they remember it at all.

We tend to think of inflation as something that happens in Zimbabwe, Argentina, or Venezuela. It doesn't happen to us.

However, even the tame 2% inflation we've experienced in 2019 could ruin your retirement Spending Plan.

Over a "normal" twenty-five-year retirement, age 65 to age 90 for example, the purchasing value of a $1,000 per month fixed income will decline to $603 per month at a constant 2% per year inflation rate.

Who has a fixed income? All of those fortunate souls who have company sponsored pension plans and everyone who receives income from a fixed **annuity**.

A cost of living adjustment increases Social Security every year. The formula intentionally increases payouts by less than annual **CPI** inflation.

How much less? It seems to vary, but it's been running about a half percent (0.5%) less than CPI since 2008.

Even this 0.5% difference would shrink the value of $1,000 in monthly Social Security income to $882 over the same twenty-five-years.

Now suppose you retire at 55 and live to 105.

Oops! The purchasing power of your pension and **annuity** income declined from $1,000 per month to $364. Your $1,000 monthly Social Security purchasing power declined to $778.

This is not good. You'll feel the pinch long before the end of your retirement.

Clearly, you need a strategy that increases your income to compensate for inflation-caused losses in purchasing power.

Let's assume you start your retirement at 65 and experience the "tame" 2% inflation rate. Your initial monthly income is $3,000. Broken down as follows.

1. Social Security = $1,000 per month
2. Pension = $1,000 per month
3. Withdrawals from Your Nest Egg = $1,000 per month

Ten years later you can expect your purchasing power to break out this way.

1. Social Security = $951
2. Pension = $817
3. Nest Egg Withdrawal = $1,000 (you plan to increase withdrawals to keep up with inflation)

So, after ten years, when you're 75, your effective monthly income (purchasing power) is $951 + $817 + $1,000 = $2,768. This is 8% less than at the start.

How does this effect you? In order to maintain your standard of living you want to make up the purchasing power lost to inflation every year.

In the example, you already increase your Nest Egg withdrawals by the 2% inflation rate. That's how you maintain your $1,000 monthly purchasing power from the Nest Egg portion of your income.

Your pension is fixed. You'll have to replace that 2% annual loss from another source, probably your Nest Egg. That implies increasing your Nest Egg withdrawals by 4% per year.

Social Security is what it is, at least for now. If it continues to fall behind CPI inflation by 0.5% per year, you'll need to replace that shortfall too.

Your annual withdrawals from your Nest Egg must rise to 4.5% (2% + 2% + 0.5%). Your Nest Egg has to grow 4.5% per year just to stay even.

The more your initial retirement income relies on pensions, annuities, and Social Security, the bigger this problem becomes.

A higher inflation rate will increase the problem. And inflation could get much higher,

At 4% annual inflation, for example, pension purchasing power would decline over ten years from $1,000 to $665.

Even if Social Security COLAs (Cost of Living Adjustments) continue growing at 0.5% less than CPI, your Nest Egg withdrawals must increase by 8.5% per year to maintain your monthly purchasing power. And, it's not at all certain the Social Security COLA would be that high.

Inflation must be taken into account. We'll look at how to do it in "Managing Investments".

Hyperinflation

What about hyperinflation? Or just high inflation?

"In 1956, Phillip Cagan wrote The Monetary Dynamics of Hyperinflation, the book often regarded as the first serious study of hyperinflation and its effects.... In his book, Cagan defined a hyperinflationary

episode as starting in the month that the monthly inflation rate exceeds 50%, and as ending when the monthly inflation rate drops below 50% and stays that way for at least a year. Economists usually follow Cagan's description that hyperinflation occurs when the monthly inflation rate exceeds 50%."

From Wikipedia.com, 2019

Hyperinflation of more than 50% per month is an event approaching the collapse of civilization.

People are reduced to barter exchanges. Wages become meaningless. Zimbabwe prints bank notes in denominations of One Trillion Zimbabwe Dollars. Businesses fail. Governments are overthrown. People die.

Take a glance at Venezuela.

Interestingly, **stocks** in companies that survive hyperinflation have been known to recover their value for those who can hold on to them. But, in the event, they won't put food on the table.

Tradable goods are the only forms of wealth that matter in these conditions.

I once read that bars of soap are among the most tradable and storable goods for use in hyperinflation barter transactions.

Perhaps, I'll invest in a case.

Hyperinflation has occurred in other countries in the past hundred years, but it hasn't happened in the United States since the Civil War. Confederate dollars rapidly lost their value and, of course, went to zero.

The United States did experience high inflation (not hyperinflation) as recently as the late 1970s and early 1980s. I remember it well.

The trending things you wanted to own then were mortgaged **real**

estate and gold. The things you wanted to sell fast were bonds and cash.

The wages of most employees failed to keep up with inflation. People had to reduce their standard of living. They had little choice. Every month their money wouldn't buy as much as it did the month before.

Corporate sales and profits shrank. Layoffs were announced nearly every day.

After a while things stabilized. That meant the economy and the stock market bounced around at a low level for years.

High inflation, or at least higher inflation, is something we're likely to see again.

Over a long retirement of many decades, it's probable.

Nothing is certain. But I'm not going to bet against seeing high inflation again in my lifetime.

I'll look at protection from high inflation in "Managing Investments".

Over-Spending

Already, I'm tempted to take an extra withdrawal from our Nest Egg to pay for a river cruise in Europe. And, I'm not even retired yet.

Clearly, I'm vulnerable to over-spending my plan.

Not to worry, I won't do it. Spending discipline is essential for our Nest Egg to support us forever.

Perhaps you won't be tempted to withdraw more money from your retirement accounts than is in your plan. If that's you – it's a wonderful thing.

I suspect most people are at least as tempted as I am. All that money is setting there. How could spending a few thousand dollars matter?

And, the truth is, if it were just once, it probably wouldn't matter. But once leads to twice, leads to three times, and so on.

What to do?

The key, I think, is to include extra money in your spending plan at the onset. You know you want to travel, buy a new boat, pay for your granddaughter's college education, whatever.

So, add money to your monthly Spending Plan. Withdraw a bit more every month and put it in a savings account earmarked for the extra spending.

Build your Spending Plan and your retirement Income Plan around all of your expenses, including the extras.

Count adding to your Emergency Fund every month, saving for vacations, and saving for other things you want to do as expenses.

Then, when you accumulate enough in the saving account, buy, do, go, or give as you wish.

It's not now or never. It's when.

That's a discipline I can live with.

The bad news is you'll need a larger Nest Egg to support the increased monthly withdrawals.

The good news is you can adjust your Integrated Retirement Plan in advance to prepare for it.

Over-spending your plan will put your forever retirement at risk.

The combination of over-spending your plan and failing to prepare for inflation leads to going broke - gradually, and then suddenly.

Market Risk

Markets go up and down. About 80% of the time the stock markets go up. When they go up, people cheer.

Sometimes they go down a lot in a short time. This is known as a "crash".

Sometimes they go down for an extended period of time; generally called a "bear market".

Sometimes they go down a little for a short time; a "correction".

Always, markets fluctuate.

All markets crash. When they'll crash is unknowable.

Markets also recover. When they'll recover is equally unknowable.

Economist John Maynard Keynes said, *"Markets can remain irrational for longer than you can remain **solvent**."*

Predicting when markets will turn up or down is a fool's errand. No one does it successfully, except occasionally, by accident.

Preparing for and dealing with a crash requires a combination of Investing Strategy, Asset Allocation, and Behavioral Psychology.

I'll work through these in the Managing Investments section.

Catastrophe

Catastrophes take many forms. They can be:

1. Acts of God
2. Acts of War
3. Acts of Congress
4. Acts of Judges
5. Acts of Criminals.

There's no point wasting breath on any form of Apocalypse; Zombies,

Asteroids striking the Earth, EMPs, Solar Flares, or the general collapse of civilization. Retirement and Financial Independence are meaningless in these circumstances.

So, let's consider lesser catastrophes. Catastrophes that leave civilization intact but still have the potential to derail your retirement.

Acts of God:

You can protect yourself from Acts of God, i.e. Natural Disasters or Loss of Physical or Mental Abilities.

Standard insurance policies such as health, home owner's, and personal property insurance policies are the simplest and most effective protection.

It also helps to **diversify** your money across **asset classes**, investment companies, and geographies.

Legal contingencies for handling your financial affairs may be necessary if you're incapacitated, even temporarily. Trusts and Powers of Attorney are examples of useful legal contingencies.

1) Natural Disasters

Hurricanes, earthquakes, and other natural disasters are local phenomena.

In addition to buying insurance, businesses protect themselves from natural disasters by duplicating data and capacity in alternate locations. The idea is that a disaster in Michigan is unlikely to affect a facility in Texas.

Duplication doesn't ensure the business will continue running without a hitch. Only that it can continue to run.

The same can be said for your retirement. A tornado that destroys your home, leaving your family alive and well, is a disaster. But, if you have the proper insurance, and you have assets you can reach quickly, the disaster doesn't have to destroy your retirement.

2) Loss of Physical or Mental Abilities

Serious illness or accident can threaten your retirement.

Medical care can drain financial resources. Beyond that, your decision-making ability could be impaired.

You could find yourself physically unable to speak. You could be unconscious.

Severe pain could disrupt your ability to think clearly.

Clinical depression or other debilitating mental illness could leave you vulnerable.

The utility of health insurance under these circumstances is without question. But how will you protect your ability to make good decisions?

A trusted partner with power of attorney may be the only real solution. Better to think this through and set up the appropriate documents now. It would be best to talk this over with an Estate Attorney.

With luck you'll never need the documents – it's just insurance.

Acts of War:

A war that sweeps over your land and family might as well be the apocalypse.

Although, even in this case, it's possible to protect your family to some degree.

You can have assets in other geographical locations, including other countries. Perhaps enough to allow your family to escape the destruction, even to thrive in a new location.

Lesser Acts of War might be more like terrorist attacks. Their effect on your family and retirement will resemble the Acts of God discussed previously. Your defense is the same.

Acts of Congress:

It's more difficult to protect yourself from Acts of Congress.

You can, however, diversify your money across different legal constructs.

For example, you can have money in a Roth IRA, a Traditional IRA, in a non-tax-deferred brokerage account, in real estate, annuities, precious metal coins, and cash. You can keep some in foreign bank accounts. You can hold **precious metals** overseas. And, you can own foreign real estate.

Congress is unlikely to ruin all of those constructs at the same time.

If you trust Congress to act in your best interests, please reread my Mother's health insurance story.

When Congress acts, some win and some lose. Even Congress doesn't know which is which. They probably didn't read the bill anyway.

The good news is Congress usually acts slowly. If you're paying attention, you might see the Congressional train bearing down on you. You might have time to get out of the way.

You can get out of the way faster if you already have methods set up to transfer money from one legal place to another.

For example, link your investment accounts with bank accounts. A link to an off-shore bank account wouldn't hurt either.

. . .

Acts of Judges:

Various forms of **liability** insurance are helpful to protect yourself from the Acts of Judges (the Courts). Auto liability insurance is a must, of course. Umbrella insurance that covers you from other possible liability threats (possible civil suits) should be considered.

Some protection is available from holding your activities or assets most vulnerable to law suits in an LLC (Limited Liability Corporation).

Virginia, where I live, charges $50 a year to maintain LLC registration.

Liability isn't the only way the Courts threaten your retirement. Real estate can be confiscated with or without compensation.

The state might decide their next freeway must run through the middle of your house.

Your backyard could be declared "wetlands" effectively taking it from you. You won't be able to do anything with it ever again.

In 1933, the United States government confiscated gold coins and bullion held by citizens.

The government paid for the gold at the official rate of $20 per ounce. When they finished rounding it up, they arbitrarily raised the official price of gold to $35 an ounce. Effectively, the government stole $15 an ounce from the previous owners.

Once again, diversification across asset classes and countries can limit the damage.

Acts of Criminals.:

Your greatest single vulnerability to financial catastrophe is identity theft.

The internet is a sieve. All of your investment accounts are held as ones and zeros in computers at various financial institutions.

There are simple things you can do to reduce the odds of identity theft. But there's nothing you can do to prevent it completely.

- What You Can Do

1. Use complex passwords.
2. Use two-factor identity verification.
3. Periodically change your passwords.
4. Don't use the same password for all of your accounts.
5. Don't use "public" computers.
6. Do use a VPN when accessing the internet through public WiFi hotspots.
7. Don't open emails from unknown or suspicious sources.
8. Read emails with skepticism – if your friend sends you something out of character, assume it's a virus.
9. Don't open suspicious hyperlinks, even from your friends.
10. Consider using an identity protection service, like LifeLock

All of the above are standard, IT (Information Technology) security advice. I didn't make them up.

All of them help. None of them guarantee the safety of your investment accounts.

Some financial planners advise people to consolidate their investment accounts and their savings accounts. Make it simple, they say.

I get it. Simple is nice.

Simple has a downside though. Fewer accounts and financial institutions mean more of your Nest Egg is vulnerable to a single hack. Spreading your money over several financial institutions means only a portion of your Nest Egg is vulnerable to a single hack.

It's simplicity versus security. Find your own compromise.

There are still burglars, of course. But, as long as your family is unharmed, the damage a home invasion can do to your finances is limited. Just don't keep your Nest Egg under your mattress. And do cover your belongings with a personal property insurance policy.

If you suffer a burglary, it'll be a hardship. It may cause emotional trauma. But it won't ruin your retirement.

TEN

Managing Investments

You've reviewed the risks to your retirement. Some of them should be dealt with by purchasing insurance. Some by diversifying financial institutions, legal constructs, and countries. And there's a real need to plan for the possibility your judgement may become impaired.

After **mitigating** (minimizing as much as possible) those risks, you're left with risks that can only be **mitigated** in the markets. These risks require managing your investments.

I propose the following objectives for managing your investments:

1. Protection from a permanent loss caused by a market crash or "bear market".
2. Protection from the loss of purchasing power caused by periods of high inflation.
3. Protection from the **long-term** loss of purchasing power caused by sustained low inflation.
4. Protection from "sequence of returns" risk.
5. Protection from adverse regulations and laws.
6. Allow for Future Lifestyle Improvements

Protection from a Bear Market or Market Crash

Most financial advisers recommend a "buy and hold" long term investing strategy. They believe this strategy consistently outperforms active trading or any attempts at market timing.

"Buy and hold, also called position trading, is an investment strategy where an investor buys stocks and holds them for a long time, with the goal that stocks will gradually increase in value over a long period of time.

This is based on the view that in the long run financial markets give a good rate of return even while taking into account a degree of volatility. Buy-and-hold says that investors will never see such returns if they bail out after a decline. This viewpoint holds that market timing (i.e. the concept that one can enter the market on the lows and sell on the highs), does not work; attempting such timing gives negative results, at least for small or unsophisticated investors, so it is better for them to simply buy and hold."

Wikipedia, 2019

The Behavioral Psychology Problem

There is a problem with "buy and hold". The problem is the well-documented poor behavior of investors. When markets fall, they sell.

When markets are calm or rising, investors believe they have a higher risk tolerance than they really do.

When calm, they believe they have the courage to ride it out when the market falls and they're faced with losses.

When times are good, it's easy to convince yourself you have the intestinal fortitude (guts) to tolerate any crash or correction.

But, when the value of your Nest Egg has fallen 25% in a month, and it continues falling daily, things feel different. You're in free-fall. You desperately want a parachute.

You sell – low.

Many books and papers describe in detail the strong tendency for investors to sell when their investments fall in value.

"We don't have to look too far to find ample evidence of poor investor behavior on a wide scale. In 1999 when the dot-com bubble got bigger and bigger, the NASDAQ was up over 85 percent...FOR THE YEAR. That was crazy enough, but what happened in the first quarter of 2000 was insane. We went on a buying binge, all of us. Up until January 2000, the record for net inflows (money going in, minus money going out) into stock mutual funds was $29 billion. Now here we were in January 2000, right after an 86 percent run up. Look at these numbers.

In January $44.5 billion poured into stock mutual funds.

In February, the shortest month of the year, inflows hit $55.6 billion. That's almost $2 billion a day!

And March was nothing to sneeze at either with an investment of another $39.9 billion.

Think about it. Over three months, $140 billion entered the market— AFTER it already had gained over 80 percent. At a time when we should have shown some caution, we allowed ourselves to get swept along with the crowd, and we paid for it. March 24, 2000, was the peak of the dot-com bubble, and by October 2002 the market had lost 50 percent of its value. So, had we poured money in, just in time to get our heads taken off!

If the behavior at the top was wild, clearly, we still hadn't learned the *lesson on the way down. With the S&P 500 down over 50 percent from its highs, we couldn't sell fast enough. October marked the fifth month in a row that investors pulled more money out of stock mutual funds than they invested. That had never happened. I repeat, never. October turned out to be the market low. So, at the market low, instead of buying equities at the best "sale" prices in five years, investors moved their money into bond funds, making the classic mistake of having bought high and sold low. Bond funds experienced a record inflow of $140 billion in 2002, at a time when bonds were at 46-year highs."*

"Buying High and Selling Low"

https://www.iwillteachyoutoberich.com/blog/the-psychology-of-buying-high-and-selling-low/

And yet, those intrepid souls who ride out the crashes and corrections are rewarded.

"A news item that has gotten a lot of attention recently concerned an internal performance review of Fidelity accounts to determine which type of investors received the best returns between 2003 and 2013. The customer account audit revealed that the best investors were either dead or inactive—the people who switched jobs and "forgot" about an old 401(k) leaving the current options in place, or the people who died and the assets were frozen while the estate handled the assets. ...

My speculation on why dead people beat everyone else is that there is no temptation to employ recency bias and sell a stock simply because the price of the company went down or they assume that the recent bad economic conditions will continue perpetually into the future."

"Fidelity's Best Investors Are Dead"

https://theconservativeincomeinvestor.com/fidelitys-best-investors-are-dead/

. . .

Wow! It looks like most of those intrepid souls were dead, or at least uninterested.

The financial advisers who recommend "buy and hold", know the greatest value they bring to clients is their ability to talk clients out of panic-induced selling.

When the advisor reminds the client of the historical success of "buy and hold" and the long-term nature of the client's financial plan, sometimes they can "talk them off the ledge". Sometimes, they can keep them invested through the crash and recovery.

Of course, advisors aren't always successful in talking clients off the ledge.

More importantly, if you're reading this, you don't have a financial advisor. You're not paying someone thousands of dollars per year to hold your hand through the market drawdowns.

You're on your own.

But, here's one thing you should not do. You should not assume you're different.

If you had the staying power of Warren Buffet, you'd be rich already.

Instead, to weather the market drawdowns, you need an investing strategy you can execute through good times and bad. A strategy you believe in. One that gives you conviction.

This is possible. But it's not "buy and hold".

If you're interested in a deeper dive into investor behavior, I recommend these books.

1. "The Laws of Wealth: Psychology and the secret to investing success", by Daniel Crosby

2. "The Little Book of Behavioral Investing: How not to be your own worst enemy", by James Montier

And my own contribution.

"Why You Are the Greatest Obstacle to Your Investing Success: The Clear Thinking Short Version" by Mel Clark

Strategies You Can Believe In

There are three basic strategies you can use to prote

They don't provide absolute safety. They do reduce drawdowns, making them less painful.

They also position you to take advantage of the eventual recovery.

1. Time Diversification
2. Asset Allocation with Rebalancing
3. Trend Following with Trailing Stops

I use all three.

Most of our Nest Egg is protected using Time Diversification and Asset Allocation with Rebalancing. I recommend these strategies without reservation.

Trend Following requires more work, engagement, and discipline. You really have to love the markets and follow them daily to do it right.

Eventually, I'll publish a book describing my particular method of Trend Following. But I'm not going to recommend Trend Following or discuss it further in this book.

Time Diversification

Diversifying your Nest Egg over time is a little like having a giant emergency fund.

The purpose of an emergency fund is to give you a temporary "fudge factor". A cash reserve to cover emergency expenses beyond your normal budget.

Monthly contributions to the emergency fund are part of your budget. Irregular large withdrawals to pay for occasional surprise expenses are not.

Effectively, emergency funds provide for the certainty of financial emergencies by spreading their cost over many months.

A credit card would do the same. The difference is that with the emergency fund you pay in advance and earn interest. With the credit card, you pay after the fact and pay interest.

The emergency fund is a source of freedom. The credit card is a prison.

Time Diversification differs from an Emergency Fund in one main particular. It protects you from investing emergencies instead of spending emergencies.

- How to Do It

Diversifying your Nest Egg over time means dividing it up into parts with different degrees of safety and different degrees of **expected return** (growth + dividends).

You hold the money you'll need soon in the form of cash or "near cash". Your near cash is safe in the short-term. But inflation will destroy it over time. It won't grow and it'll pay only a small amount of interest or dividends.

Another portion of your Nest Egg will be in long-term investments with much higher expected **returns**. This will provide protection from long-term inflation with correspondingly higher **short-term** risks due to market fluctuations.

Two divisions are enough to explain the concept. For many people, two are enough to make it work. Some folks choose to hold an intermediate portion as well. An intermediate portion splits the difference between long-term and short-term.

Your time-diversified Nest Egg assigns money needed in the short-term to the portion protected from short-term risk. It assigns money needed in the long-term to the portion best protected from long-term risk.

What then, is the definition of short-term versus long-term?

The difference between long and short term is subjective. Recoveries from crashes and bear markets are not all alike. They don't follow the same patterns.

Most of the time markets regain their pre-crash peaks in less than three years. However, there have been recoveries that took twenty-five years to return to their pre-crash levels.

The Japanese stock market today, in 2019 - thirty years later, hasn't recovered its pre-1989 crash level.

So, what's the answer? Most people end up with their short-term portion valued at between one-year and five-years' worth of need.

"Need" is defined as the amount needed from the Nest Egg to supplement your income over a specific time period.

For example, if you need $1,000 per month to supplement your other income sources, you would need $12,000 from your Nest Egg to cover one-year and $60,000 to cover five-years.

The inability to be definite about how much should be in the short-term portion drives some people to use the third, intermediate portion.

Adding the intermediate portion, you can minimize the short-term commitment. You size the intermediate portion to cover the gap between your short-term and long-term portions.

If your short-term portion is in a bank savings account or a money market account, your intermediate portion might be invested in bonds or bank CD's (certificates of deposits).

You might have a year's worth of need in the short-term portion and three years' need in the intermediate portion.

The balance of your Nest Egg is in long-term investments. **Securities** with higher **volatility** and subject to the whims of the market.

Having a total of four years' worth of need in "safe" short-term investments gives you greater peace of mind and allows you to ride out all but the very worst bear markets without touching your long-term funds.

And that's really the point. The short-term plus the intermediate term portions of your Nest Egg allow you to let your long-term portion fall with the bear market and then recover without making withdrawals while the market is down.

It gives you time to wait for the recovery before resuming withdrawals.

Just knowing you have this cushion increases your confidence and your ability to maintain your long-term investment strategy, whatever it is.

- How I Do It

The Time Diversification strategy my wife and I use consists of holding an extra-large Emergency Fund in an interest-bearing bank account. It's bigger than I'd prefer. But it makes my wife feel safe.

Soon, we may move most of it to a diversified **mutual fund** account to generate additional dividend income.

. . .

Asset Allocation with Rebalancing

"In fact, broad diversification and rebalancing have been shown to add half a percentage point of performance per year."

"The Laws of Wealth: Psychology and the secret to investing success" by Daniel Crosby

Diversifying the long-term portion of your Nest Egg over a number of **uncorrelated** asset classes reduces drawdowns and increases long-term returns.

What the heck does that mean?

Modern Portfolio Theory (MPT):

"Modern portfolio theory (MPT) is a theory on how risk-averse investors can construct portfolios to optimize or maximize expected return based on a given level of market risk, emphasizing that risk is an inherent part of higher reward. According to the theory, it's possible to construct an "efficient frontier" of optimal portfolios offering the maximum possible expected return for a given level of risk. This theory was pioneered by Harry Markowitz in his paper "Portfolio Selection," published in 1952 by the Journal of Finance. He was later awarded a Nobel prize for developing the MPT."

https://www.investopedia.com/terms/m/modernportfoliotheory.asp, 2019

There's a lot of math behind the theory. Calculating and maintaining the optimum **portfolio** for a particular risk profile is too complex for me. I leave it to professional money managers.

I need something simple. Something that doesn't require a lot of math, data, or time.

You can get 80% of the benefit of MPT by

1. Putting together a portfolio of four or more uncorrelated asset classes.
2. Assigning an **allocation** to each **asset class**. This means deciding what percentage of your Nest Egg you'll commit to each asset class.
3. Selecting specific securities to represent each asset class.
4. Buying the selected securities in accordance with your allocation assignments.
5. Periodically rebalancing the securities back to the assigned allocations.

Over long periods of time, this process does better than "buy and hold". And, it reduces drawdown**s**.

"the most ironclad rule I have been able to find studying masses of data on the stock market, both in the United States and developed foreign markets, is the idea of reversion to the mean."

James O'Shaughnessy as quoted in

"The Laws of Wealth: Psychology and the secret to investing success" by Daniel Crosby

"In 1998, Larry Summers of Harvard and James Porterba of MIT published a seminal paper titled 'Mean Reversion in Stock Prices: Evidence and Implications'. They set out to examine the returns to NYSE stocks from 1926 to 1985, to understand the after-effects of large increases or decreases in price. As you may now expect, they found that periods of exceptionally high returns were followed by periods of low returns and vice versa."

"The Laws of Wealth: Psychology and the secret to investing success" by Daniel Crosby

Better **returns** come from selling assets when they're relatively high and buying them when they're relatively low. This isn't market timing. It's also not an all-in proposition.

You don't predict which way the market will move or when. You don't make forecasts of any kind.

Instead, you react to actual market moves (price changes) using pre-established, and preferably written rules.

You assume markets fluctuate. And that, eventually, they "**revert to the mean**".

You sell a specific, measured amount of an asset that has risen in value, Asset Class A. By selling, you bring the value of Asset Class A back to the **allocation** percentage you established.

You then buy a specific, measured amount of an asset that has fallen in value, Asset Class B. Buying brings the value of this asset class back to its allocation percentage.

Over time both asset classes "**revert to the mean**". The one you sold, Asset Class A, falls in price and the one you bought, Asset Class B, rises.

Eventually, the situation completely reverses. Your rule tells you to buy a measured portion of Asset Class A and sell Asset Class B.

Over the course of these transactions, you make a profit on both asset classes. The overall value of your portfolio will increase by the amount of the two profits, even if the prices of the two asset classes ends up precisely where they started.

This is the concept you use in taking advantage of MPT. Let's dig into the details.

. . .

Asset Allocation:

As mentioned earlier, Asset Allocation means

(1) selecting the asset classes and specific securities to represent them;

(2) assigning a specific percentage of the value of your portfolio (Nest Egg) to each asset class;

(3) buying the selected securities in accordance with the assigned percentages.

Below is an example of what is known as "The Permanent Portfolio"

"For the money you need to take care of you for the rest of your life, set up a simple, balanced, diversified portfolio. I call this a "Permanent Portfolio" because once you set it up, you never need to rearrange the investment mix— even if your outlook for the future changes. The portfolio should assure that your wealth will survive any event — including an event that would be devastating to any individual element within the portfolio... It isn't difficult or complicated to have such a portfolio this safe. You can achieve a great deal of diversification with a surprisingly simple portfolio. "

"The Permanent Portfolio", by Harry Browne

Harry Browne's Permanent Portfolio consists of four asset classes equally weighted at 25% each. The four asset classes are:

1. Stocks = 25%
2. Bonds = 25%
3. Precious Metals = 25%
4. Cash = 25%

The asset classes, in our example, are represented by these **EFTs (Exchange Traded Funds).**

1. Stocks = iShares Core S&P Total Market ETF, **Ticker Symbol** = ITOT.
2. Bonds = iShares 20+ yr. Treasury Bond ETF, Ticker TLT.
3. Precious Metals = iShares Gold Trust ETF, Ticker IAU.
4. Cash = iShares 1-3 yr. Treasury Bond ETF, Ticker SHY.

If the example Nest Egg value starts out at $100,000, then you buy the following to establish your Permanent Portfolio allocations.

1. ITOT = $25,000 (100,000 * 0.25 = 25,000)
2. TLT = $25,000 (100,000 * 0.25 = 25,000)
3. IAU = $25,000 (100,000 * 0.25 = 25,000)
4. SHY = $25,000 (100,000 * 0.25 = 25,000)

For additional information on Asset Allocation and thoughts on how to choose your allocations, refer to my earlier book, "What Is Asset Allocation?".

Rebalancing:

Almost immediately after you buy the selected securities, your portfolio will get out of balance.

Markets fluctuate. The values of the securities in your portfolio go up and down.

Their current values will no longer represent the percentage allocations you picked (in the example, the allocations of The Permanent Portfolio).

If you don't occasionally realign your individual security values with your portfolio allocations (**rebalance**), you will not reap the benefits of MPT.

Eventually, your portfolio will be dominated by one of the asset classes. You will be **exposed** to the risk of a crash in that asset.

Without rebalancing, there is no systematic selling high and buying low. You fail to take the many small profits found in fluctuating markets.

Rebalancing is the other essential half of Asset Allocation.

Timing of Rebalancing:

Timing rebalancing is not timing the market. It's simply rebalancing your portfolio on a predetermined schedule or plan.

Rebalancing can be successful and useful on almost any schedule. Some of the great **institutional investors** rebalance their portfolios continuously.

Most individual investors **rebalance** once a year. Some rebalance every other year. Others, once a quarter.

There are also people, like me, who rebalance when their positions change by some minimum (threshold) amount. Robo Advisors, such as Betterment, tend to use this timing as well.

The key to timing your rebalancing is to establish a system and then use it with discipline.

Your system could be as simple as, "I rebalance my portfolio every year on my birthday."

It could be a system as complicated as mine, with a formula built into a spreadsheet that signals when a security is more than 1% out of alignment with its allocation percentage.

It doesn't matter. Establish a rebalancing timing system and stick to it. That matters.

. . .

The Mechanics of Rebalancing:

There are three basic cases. Each rebalancing case has a slightly different method.

Case 1 – Money is added to the account.

Case 2 – Money is withdrawn from the account.

Case 3 – Money is neither added nor withdrawn, but the market changed the relative values of the portfolio positions.

In Case 1 you identify the one or two securities most below their allocations. Then you use the new money you are adding to the account to buy those securities. This increases their **position** value by the amount of the purchases.

In Case 2 you identify the one or two securities most above their allocations. Sell the amounts of those securities sufficient to generate the required cash withdrawal. This reduces their position values moving them back toward their allocations.

Case 3 is the situation I referred to earlier. You're not putting money in or taking it out. You just need to realign the positions with their allocation percentages.

So, in Case 3 you identify the securities above their allocations (above their thresholds) and those below their allocations. Then sell enough of the "too high" securities to bring them back into alignment. Use the money released to buy more of the "too low" securities.

If your portfolio is entirely in one mutual fund account, you can usually "**exchange**" money from one fund in a family of mutual funds to another in the same family without paying a commission. An exchange combines the selling and buying transactions into one event.

. . .

Transaction Costs:

Rebalancing your portfolio has costs.

First, there's the cost of your time and attention. Even if you only rebalance on your birthday or whatever anniversary date you choose, you have to do the little bit of work involved.

Second, if you hold your portfolio in a traditional brokerage account, you might have to pay a commission for every buy and sell transaction. This could range from $1.00 to $15.00 per **trade**.

Third, use of a **Robo Advisor** or a "**balanced fund**", either a mutual fund or an ETF, will entail a management fee higher than those charged by "index funds".

More detail on how to rebalance is available in my book, "How to Rebalance Your Portfolio".

Stay the Course:

The Asset Allocation with Rebalancing strategy improves your ability to "stay the course".

When markets crash and portfolio values sink, investors get anxious. Nearly everyone sells close to the bottom – close to the lowest prices.

Perhaps the greatest benefit human financial advisors bring to their clients is the ability to soothe their fears during the market's scary times.

When financial advisors succeed in keeping their clients from selling during the downturn, they save their clients many times what they charge in fees.

But you and I don't have financial advisors. We need a way to "stay the course" without help.

Asset Allocation with Rebalancing boosts your ability to "stay the course" in three ways.

1. Your portfolio value falls less than the market. It may still fall a lot, maybe 25% instead of 50%. But it's less of a fall than others experience. So, your anxiety level isn't quite as high.
2. When you're anxious, you want to "do something". You feel compelled to take action to relieve the stress.

Asset Allocation with Rebalancing gives you something to do. If fact, if you're using the change in a threshold value as your rebalancing trigger, your system requires you to do something. It tells you to buy more of the securities that have fallen most in value and to sell some of those that have risen (or fallen the least).

This is counter to what others are doing. It's counter to what you probably want to do. But it's the right thing to do. And, your system is telling you to do it. You can take action and still comply with your system discipline. You can "do something" and feel good about it afterward.

Finally, simply having a strategy that you know works gives you confidence. You know you'll weather the downturn. Even benefit from it.

You can stay the course and be better off when the market recovers.

It will, of course, recover.

Protection from Loss of Purchasing Power Caused by High Inflation

Protecting your Nest Egg from high inflation is a matter of carefully choosing the asset classes for your portfolio.

Let's look again at the four asset classes in Harry Browne's Permanent Portfolio They are:

1. Stocks = 25%
2. Bonds = 25%
3. Precious Metals = 25%
4. Cash = 25%

- Stocks

In the long-run, stocks have provided excellent inflation protection. Eventually, businesses adjust their cost structures and prices to the new inflationary environment.

Stock prices eventually reflect the adjustments. Your capital is preserved, and growth continues.

However, in the short-run, companies have difficulty. At the beginning of a time of high inflation, they can't raise their prices as fast as their costs increase. Their customers just won't tolerate it.

Customers incomes go up, but they rise slower than their costs. Almost always their increases in income will lag their increasing costs by months, even years. In most cases, customers are forced to reduce spending. They buy less.

So, in the short-run, stock prices tend to fall. As does the value of your portfolio.

- Bonds

Rising inflation usually means rising interest rates. Rising interest rates causes the prices of bonds to fall. This reduces the value of your portfolio.

An exception is created when the FED (Federal Reserve Bank) forces short-term interest rates downward in an attempt to forestall a recession.

However, in a high inflation environment, the FED is likely to try to reduce the inflation rate by increasing short-term interest rates. They did precisely this in the 1980s with great success.

There is also a special class of US Government Bonds called TIPS (Treasury Inflation-Protected Securities).

"Treasury Inflation-Protected Security (TIPS) is a Treasury bond that is indexed to inflation to protect investors from the negative effects of rising prices. The principal value of TIPS rises as inflation rises. Inflation is the pace at which prices increase throughout the U.S. economy as measured by the Consumer Price Index or CPI."

https://www.investopedia.com/terms/t/tips.asp

TIPS provide inflation protection by design. Other bonds do not.

- Precious Metals

The price of gold, and the other precious metals, generally keeps up with inflation. Often gold goes up faster in times of high inflation. People buy it in anticipation of more and even higher inflation.

Gold is the traditional safe haven. The place people park their money to protect it from the stupidity of governments. And, high inflation is always caused by the stupidity of a government.

- Cash

The fourth Permanent Portfolio asset class is cash. By definition, cash is the target of high inflation. It loses its purchasing power with every point of inflation.

If you were invested in the Permanent Portfolio under high inflation you could expect the general trends outlined below.

Keep in mind, they are just general trends or tendencies. They are not laws of nature or even predictions. Actual events will differ in unknown ways from these tendencies.

Nevertheless, here are the tendencies.

Initially, your stocks would fall. After some months they would likely stabilize. Eventually, they would recover.

Initially, interest rates rise and your bonds fall in value. After some months, interest rates and values stabilize. Eventually, inflation is tamed and interest rates slowly come back down. It could take years, but in the end, your bonds recover. The exception is TIPS bonds. They will rise in value with inflation from the very beginning.

Initially, your precious metals rise. Perhaps a lot. As inflation is tamed, the price of precious metals will stabilize. If the price of gold increased by a lot more than inflation, you should expect it to fall and stabilize somewhere around parity with its original purchasing power. That is, its final price will be close to its starting price plus the accumulated inflation.

The purchasing power of your cash position is permanently eroded by the total accumulated inflation, less whatever amount of interest you earned. If you held the cash in short-term Treasuries or Money Market Funds, there's a chance your interest rate increased enough to minimize your loss of purchasing power.

If you trigger rebalancing when an asset value changes by a threshold amount, you would rebalance as your stocks and bonds fall. Probably several times.

You would most likely sell gold and cash and buy stocks and bonds.

Later, during the recovery, you may be triggered several times to sell stocks and bonds and buy back into gold and cash.

Thus, you earn a profit on the whole.

Beyond the Permanent Portfolio, other asset classes useful in high inflationary times include real estate, fine art, other **commodities** (copper, wheat, coffee, etc) and other **collectables** (rare coins and stamps for example).

As you can see, the key to reducing the damage from high inflation is a careful selection of the asset classes you hold in your portfolio.

You need some **exposure** to asset classes that go up with inflation. This mostly means precious metals, other commodities, and TIPS.

Real estate is hard. Owning actual physical property is certainly possible. But it requires other skill sets. And a lot of time and attention.

The conventional way to invest in real estate through financial instruments is to buy shares in REITs (Real Estate Investment Trusts). These are really special classes of stocks.

They are companies subject to the same problems as other companies during high inflation. Plus, they have unique problems with high inflation. Some of their customers default or go out of business. Others move because they can't pay higher rents. The REITs usually carry a lot of mortgage and other debt that must be paid regardless of the state of their customers.

Consequently, the REITs may do worse than the market. It's not at all clear they would provide the necessary protection.

Fine art and other collectables are good choices if you have the skills and knowledge to **trade** them. I don't.

For me, inflation protection means an allocation to precious metals – and maybe TIPS.

- Bitcoin

I hear some of you asking, "What about Bitcoin? What about cryptocurrencies?"

I admit to playing with Bitcoin, Ethereum, Litecoin, and a couple of other cryptocurrencies too.

I've noticed they tend to follow the direction of the gold price. When gold goes up Bitcoin tends to go up. When gold goes down Bitcoin tends to go down. It's just a tendency, though. The cryptos also zig and zag significantly independent of the price of gold.

For now, there just isn't enough history for me to commit a serious amount of money to crypto. I hold a small amount of several cryptos as long-term speculations. I also Trend Follow the Bitcoin Trust, GBTC. I don't consider this money part of my Nest Egg. My wife calls it, "Play Money."

Protection from Sustained Low Inflation

Sustained low inflation is easier to mitigate. Don't ignore it though. In the long run, it's dangerous.

Inevitably the purchasing power of cash, earning little interest, will be destroyed. To protect your Nest Egg from this threat you need to grow it faster than the inflation rate.

You can't rely on gold or other precious metals to increase faster than sustained low inflation. They're **volatile**. They're subject to price changes driven by supply and demand. By fear and by greed.

This is true of all securities. But gold is especially affected because of its long-standing role as the money of last resort.

Historically, bonds have paid interest greater than the inflation rate. In recent years, however, intervention by the FED and other central banks around the world has disconnected bond interest from inflation.

Right now, in 2019, the bonds of many developed countries have negative interest rates. Others pay interest at or near zero percent. The United States is among a select few developed countries with **sovereign bonds** paying near the rate of inflation.

Even US bonds are just keeping up with inflation or are paying slightly less.

Once again, TIPS are the exception. Their values keep up with inflation and they have a small **dividend yield** too.

Stocks are the winner in this category. The prices of stocks generally go up when inflation is low and steady. Plus, average dividends come close to matching inflation all by themselves.

If you have the requisite skills real estate and collectables also work under sustained low inflation.

So, the solution to sustained low inflation is a strong allocation to stocks, picking bonds that pay enough interest, and parking your cash allocation in interest-bearing securities that minimize the damage.

Protection from "Sequence of Returns" Risk

"Sequence of Returns" risk is a special case of a bear market. It's the risk that a bear happens at about the time you retire. Just when you start to depend on income from your Nest Egg.

This is a special problem because you begin drawing income from a Nest Egg reduced in value by the bear market.

Since you're making permanent withdrawals, there's a chance your Nest Egg will not completely recover.

By the time the recovery kicks in you have fewer shares than when the bear started. So, even when prices recover, the value of your Nest Egg could be less than before.

If the same bear market pattern occurs a few years after you retire, your long-term success is less threatened. Your Nest Egg continues growing during those first few years. Enough, perhaps, to more than make up for your withdrawals.

When the bear finally arrives (and it will), your Nest Egg value declines from a higher peak. And, it bottoms out at a higher low.

- Sequence of Returns Risk Example

To illustrate the difference, assume you retire this year with a Nest Egg valued at $100,000 and 100% invested in iShares Core S&P Total Market ETF, Ticker Symbol = ITOT.

ITOT; Price on 7/31/2019 = $68.44 per Share, Dividends = $1.304 Dividends per Share per Year; Annual Dividend Yield = 1.91%

If the market continues to go up at 8% per year for the next three years, ITOT continues to pay 1.91%, and you withdraw $4,000 per year for current income, your portfolio values will change roughly as shown below (8% + 1.91% = 9.91%).

Year One Ending Value (+9.91% - $4,000) = $105,910

Year Two Ending Value (+9.91% - $4,000) = $112,406

Year Three Ending Value (+9.91% - $4,000) = $119,545

If in Year Four the market suffers a 30% decline, your Nest Egg value at the end of the fourth year including dividends is (-30% + 1.91% = -28.09%)

Year Four Ending Value (-28.09 - $4,000) = $81,964

. . .

If the sequence of returns is reversed your year-end portfolio values would be

Year One Ending Value (-28.09% - $4,000) = $67,910

Year Two Ending Value (+9.91% - $4,000) = $70,640

Year Three Ending Value (+9.91% - $4,000) = $73,640

Year Four Ending Value (+9.91% - $4,000) = $76,938

Neither result is a happy one. Clearly, however, the $81,964 in the first example is preferable to the $76,938 in the second

Most bear markets recover within a year or so and do only a little damage.

However, once in a while, every thirty to forty years, there's a bear that takes more than a decade to recover. That can be a retirement disaster.

What to do?

Asset Allocation with Rebalancing

Once again, Asset Allocation with Rebalancing helps.

Bonds tend to go up during bear markets.

Gold may go up or down depending on what's driving the bear.

Interest rates on cash will probably go down because of intervention by the FED. But the cash is available to redeploy into stocks when rebalancing is triggered.

Stock prices are down, but dividends are down less.

Dividend yields actually go up. This means cash redeployed to buy more stocks disproportionately increases the value of your Nest Egg dividends.

That's all good.

Withdrawal Rates

Even better is to start with a Nest Egg bigger than the minimum you need to generate income.

I'm going to discuss Withdrawal Strategies later. For now, the generally accepted baseline "**Safe Withdrawal Rate**" is "The 4% Rule".

Using **the 4% Rule** you would begin your retirement by withdrawing 4% of the value of your portfolio in the first year.

You can see the tradeoffs through the example below.

- Example

We'll again use the Permanent Portfolio as an example.

Assume your total Nest Egg is valued at $100,000 and split evenly between the four Permanent Portfolio components.

Your Nest Egg consists of:

1. ITOT = $25,000 (100,000 * 0.25 = 25,000); Price on 7/31/2019 = $68.44 per Share, Dividends = $1.304 Dividends per Share per Year
2. TLT = $25,000 (100,000 * 0.25 = 25,000); Price on 7/31/2019 = $132.43 per Share, Dividends = $3.219 Dividends per Share per Year
3. IAU = $25,000 (100,000 * 0.25 = 25,000); Price on 7/31/2019 = $13.63 per Share, Dividends = $0.00 Dividends per Share per Year

4. SHY = $25,000 (100,000 * 0.25 = 25,000); Price on 7/31/2019 = $84.63 per Share, Dividends = $1.764 Dividends per Share per Year

Total Dividends are:

1. ITOT; $25,000 / $68.44per Share = 365.28 Shares; 365.28 Shares * $1.304 Dividends per Share per Year = $476.33 Dividends per Year
2. TLT; $25,000 / $132.43 per Share = 188.779 Shares; 188.779 Shares * $3.219 Dividends per Share per Year = $607.68 Dividends per Year
3. IAU; $25,000 / $13.63 per Share = 1,834.189 Shares; 1,834.189 Shares * 0 = $0.00 Dividends per Share per Year
4. SHY; $25,000 / $84.63 per Share = 295.404 Shares; 295.404 Shares * $1.764 Dividends per Share per Year = $521.09 Dividends per Year

Total Dividends = $1,605.10 per Year ($476.33 per Year + $607.68 per Year + $0.00 per Year + $521.09 per Year)

Total Dividend Yield = 1.60% ($1,605.10 / $100,000)

Average Dividends = $133.75 per Month ($1,605.10 / 12)

Annual Withdrawal Using The 4% Rule = $4,000 (100,000*.04)

Monthly Withdrawal Using the 4% Rule = $333.33 (4,000 / 12)

All of the above is useless unless you know how much you need as monthly income.

Let's assume you need $500 per month. This is more than allowed by the 4% Rule.

If you withdraw $500 per month your actual starting Withdrawal Rate is 6%.

.   .   .

$500 per Month * 12 = $6,000 per Year

$6,000 / $100,000 = 0.06 or 6.0%

The odds that your money will last thirty years drops a lot. And, what about forty or fifty years? Not likely.

To get to a high probability of making it thirty years without running out of money, you need to start with $150,000 in your Nest Egg.

$6,000 per Year / 0.04 = $150,000

The closer your monthly withdrawal amount approaches your average dividends the safer your Nest Egg will be.

Since your portfolio generates an annual dividend payout of 1.6%, this would be your Forever Safe Withdrawal Rate.

To get to the 1.6% withdrawal rate with your current portfolio you'd need an initial Nest Egg of $375,000.

$6,000 per Year / 0.016 = $375,000

That's a big jump from $100,000.

Withdrawal Strategies

In the example above, I implied you should match your withdrawal rate to your dividend rate in order to fund a "forever" retirement. I believe that.

However, you can increase your dividend rate a bit through careful selection of securities.

I lifted the suggested portfolio above, from a web site describing The Permanent Portfolio. Here's an alternative.

Instead of

Stocks = iShares Core S&P Total Market ETF, Ticker Symbol = ITOT.

ITOT; $25,000 / $68.44 per Share = 365.28 Shares; 365.28 Shares * $1.304 Dividends per Share = $476.33 Dividends per Year

You might use

Stocks = Invesco High Yield Equity Dividend Achievers ETF, Ticket Symbol = PEY

PEY; $25,000 / $18.14 per Share = 1,378.170 Shares; 1,378.170 Shares * $0.524 Dividends per Share = $722.24 Dividends per Year

Instead of

Bonds = iShares 20+ yr. Treasury Bond ETF, Ticker TLT.

TLT; $25,000 / $132.43 per Share = 188.779 Shares; 188.779 Shares * $3.219 Dividends per Share = $607.68 Dividends per Year

You might use

Bonds = Vanguard Total Bond Market **Index Fund** ETF Shares, Ticker Symbol = BND

BND; $25,000 / $83.40 per Share = 299.760 Shares; 299.760 Shares * $2.306 Dividends per Share = $691.25 Dividends per Year

Instead of

Precious Metals = iShares Gold Trust ETF, Ticker IAU.

IAU; $25,000 / $13.63 per Share = 1,834.189 Shares; 1,834.189 Shares * $0 Dividends per Share = $0.00 Dividends per Year

You might use

Precious Metals = iShares MSCI Global Gold Miners ETF, Ticker Symbol = RING

RING; $25,000 / $22.01 per Share = 1,135.847 Shares; 1,135.847 Shares * $0.188 Dividends per Share = $213.54 Dividends per Year

Instead of

Cash = iShares 1-3 yr. Treasury Bond ETF, Ticker SHY.

SHY; $25,000 / $84.63 per Share = 295.404 Shares; 295.404 Shares * $1.764 Dividends per Share = $521.09 Dividends per Year

You might use

Cash = Vanguard Short-Term Bond Index Fund ETF Shares, Ticker Symbol = BSV

BSV; $25,000 / $80.53 per Share = 310.443 Shares; 310.443 Shares * $1.761 Dividends per Share = $546.69 Dividends per Year

These changes result in dividends of

PEY = \$722.24 per Year

BND = \$691.25 per Year

RING = \$213.54 per Year

BSV = \$546.69 per Year

Total Dividends = \$2,173.72 per Year (\$722.24 + \$691.25 + \$213.54 + \$546.69)

Total Dividend Yield = 2.17% (\$2,173.72 / \$100,000)

Average Dividends = \$181.09 per Month (\$2,173.72 / 12)

To achieve a 2.17% withdrawal rate with this portfolio you'd need an initial Nest Egg of \$275,000.

\$6,000 per Year / 0.0217 = \$276,498 or rounded off – \$275,000

That's still a big jump from \$100,000, but better.

You can also play with the allocation percentages. The 25% even split of the Permanent Portfolio is simple but arbitrary.

In the quote below from Meb Faber's book, "Global Asset Allocation", Meb describes his research that shows changing the percentages doesn't matter much to overall performance.

However, the higher the proportion you commit to any single asset class, the more exposed you are to a crash in that asset. That is, the maximum **drawdown** risk is higher.

"The funny thing about all the various iterations of our 13 asset class building blocks is that you can basically simplify them into three broad

categories: stocks, bonds, and real assets. We selected one allocation from each chapter for a comparison (otherwise it wouldn't fit on one page). The criteria wasn't that sophisticated – we just tried to pick the most heralded allocation from each chapter. Once you do simplify the exposures, you can see below in Figure 40 that many of the allocations have fairly similar broad exposures. The exceptions are 60/40 and the Buffett allocations since they place zero in real assets. Note that many of the allocations were recommended to the public at different times over the years, and the later recommendations possibly benefitted from knowledge of past returns. However, as we show below, it really doesn't matter that much!

Reference to FIGURE 40 – Asset Class Broad Allocations

"Global Asset Allocation: A Survey of the World's Top Asset Allocation Strategies" by Meb Faber

"Most of the allocations moved together in a similar fashion. However, the allocations that performed the best in the inflationary 1970s then turned around and performed the worst in the disinflationary period to follow. Also not surprisingly, the Buffett and 60/40 allocations, with a lack of real assets, performed the worst during the inflationary 1970s. Even with the difference in allocations, the spread between the worst-performing allocation, the Permanent Portfolio at 4.12%, and the best, the El-Erian Portfolio at 5.67%, was only 1.84%. That is astonishing."

Reference to FIGURE 41 – Asset Class Returns, 1973-2013

"Global Asset Allocation: A Survey of the World's Top Asset Allocation Strategies" by Meb Faber

Instead of 25% equal allocations, you could use -

45% PEY = $100,000 * 0.45 = $45,000; $45,000 / $18.14 per Share =

2,480.706 Shares; 2,480.706 Shares * $0.524 Dividends per Share per Year = $1,300.00 Dividends per Year

30% BND = $100,000 * 0.30 = $30,000; $30,000 / $83.40 per Share = 359.712 Shares; 359.712 Shares * $2.306 Dividends per Share per Year = $829.50 Dividends per Year

10% RING = $100,000 * 0.10 = $10,000; $10,000 / $22.01 per Share = 454.34 Shares; 454.34 Shares * $0.188 Dividends per Share per Year = $85.42 Dividends per Year

15% BSV = $100,000 * 0.15 = $15,000; $15,000 / $80.53 per Share = 186.266 Shares; 186.266 Shares * $1.761 Dividends per Share per Year = $328.01 Dividends per Year

This results in dividends of

PEY = $1,300.00 Dividends per Year

BND = $829.50 Dividends per Year

RING = $85.42 Dividends per Year

BSV = $328.01 Dividends per Year

Total Dividends = $2,543.93 per Year ($1,300.00 + $829.50 + $85.42 + $328.01)

Total Dividend Yield = 2.54% ($2,543.93 / $100,000)

Average Dividends = $211.99 per Month ($2,543.93 / 12)

To achieve a withdrawal rate equal to the 2.54% total dividend yield with this portfolio you need an initial Nest Egg of $236,000.

$6,000 per Year / 0.0254 = $236,220 or rounded off – $236,000

·   ·   ·

It's still a lot more than $100,000. Unfortunately, more tweaking of the portfolio won't improve the situation much.

If you need to withdraw $500 per month from a $100,000 Nest Egg your actual starting Withdrawal Rate is 6% as calculated earlier.

This implies you need a Total Dividend Yield of 6% to support your forever retirement.

You could find securities that provide a 6% dividend yield. If you did you would destroy the risk mitigating properties of a diversified portfolio.

This leaves you with two methods to deal with the disparity.

1. Delay your retirement until you can build your Nest Egg up to $236,000 (plus inflation) or
2. Reduce your supplemental income need from $500 per Month down to $212 per Month.

$100,000 * 2.54% = $2,540 per Year

= $211.67 per Month or $212 per Month (rounded off)

How does the revised portfolio weather the bear market from the "sequence of returns" examples?

Obviously, because we have four securities instead of one, we have to track all four. That requires some new assumptions.

Your Nest Egg consists of

45% PEY = $100,000 * 0.45 = $45,000

30% BND = $100,000 * 0.30 = $30,000

10% RING = $100,000 * 0.10 = $10,000

15% BSV = $100,000 * 0.15 = $15,000

Dividends are not included in the returns shown below because you'll withdraw them as income. Your withdrawal rate equals your average dividend rate.

First Sequence of Returns

PEY

Year One Ending Position Value (+8%), $45,000 * 1.08 = $48,600

Year Two Ending Position Value (+8%), $48,600 * 1.08 = $52,488

Year Three Ending Position Value (+8%), $52,488 * 1.08 = $56,687

Year Four Ending Position Value (-30%), $56,687 * 0.70 = $39,681

BND

Year One Ending Position Value (+0%), $30,000 * 1.00 = $30,000

Year Two Ending Position Value (+0%), $30,000 * 1.00 = $30,000

Year Three Ending Position Value (+0%), $30,000 * 1.00 = $30,000

Year Four Ending Position Value (+10%), $30,000 * 1.10 = $33,000

RING

Year One Ending Position Value (+0%), $10,000 * 1.00 = $10,000

Year Two Ending Position Value (+0%), $10,000 * 1.00 = $10,000

Year Three Ending Position Value (+0%), $10,000 * 1.00 = $10,000

Year Four Ending Position Value (+10%), $10,000 * 1.10 = $11,000

BSV

Year One Ending Position Value (+0%), $15,000 * 1.00 = $15,000

Year Two Ending Position Value (+0%), $15,000 * 1.00 = $15,000

Year Three Ending Position Value (+0%), $15,000 * 1.00 = $15,000

Year Four Ending Position Value (+3%), $15,000 * 1.03 = $15,450

Total Portfolio Values

Year One Ending Portfolio Value = $103,600 ($48,600 + $30,000 + $10,000 + $15,000)

Year Two Ending Portfolio Value = $107,488 ($52,488 + $30,000 + $10,000 + $15,000)

Year Three Ending Portfolio Value = $111,687 ($56,687 + $30,000 + $10,000 + $15,000)

Year Four Ending Portfolio Value = $99,131 ($39,681 + $33,000 + $11,000 + $15,450)

Although your Nest Egg suffered an 11% loss from $111,687 down to $99,131 in Year Four it is only $869 less than the Year One starting position. Your forever retirement isn't threatened.

Second Sequence of Returns

PEY

Year One Ending Position Value (-30%), $45,000 * 0.70 = $31,500

Year Two Ending Position Value (+8%), $31,500 * 1.08 = $34,020

Year Three Ending Position Value (+8%), $34,020 * 1.08 = $36,742

Year Four Ending Position Value (+8%), $36,742 * 1.08 = $39,681

BND

Year One Ending Position Value (+10%), $30,000 * 1.10 = $33,000

Year Two Ending Position Value (+0%), $33,000 * 1.00 = $33,000

Year Three Ending Position Value (+0%), $33,000 * 1.00 = $33,000

Year Four Ending Position Value (+0%), $33,000 * 1.00 = $33,000

RING

Year One Ending Position Value (+10%), $10,000 * 1.10 = $11,000

Year Two Ending Position Value (+0%), $11,000 * 1.00 = $11,000

Year Three Ending Position Value (+0%), $11,000 * 1.00 = $11,000

Year Four Ending Position Value (+0%), $11,000 * 1.00 = $11,000

BSV

Year One Ending Position Value (+3%), $15,000 * 1.03 = $15,450

Year Two Ending Position Value (+0%), $15,450 * 1.00 = $15,450

Year Three Ending Position Value (+0%), $15,450 * 1.00 = $15,450

Year Four Ending Position Value (+0%), $15,450 * 1.00 = $15,450

Total Portfolio Values

Year One Ending Portfolio Value = $103,600 ($31,500 + $33,000 + $11,000 + $15,450)

Year Two Ending Portfolio Value = $107,488 ($34,020 + $33,000 + $11,000 + $15,450)

Year Three Ending Portfolio Value = $111,687 ($56,687 + $33,000 + $11,000 + $15,450)

Year Four Ending Portfolio Value = $99,131 ($39,681 + $33,000 + $11,000 + $15,450)

In Year One your Nest Egg falls to $90,950. A loss of only 9.05% because of your properly diversified portfolio. This, compared to the 30% loss down to $67,910 when your portfolio was 100% in stocks (ITOT).

By the end of Year Four, your diversified portfolio is back to $99,131 compared to $76,938 in the 100% stocks equivalent example.

Coincidentally, both "Sequence of Returns" examples using a diversified portfolio end the four years at the same value.

The assumption of zero growth in the non-stock assets during the "normal" years is arbitrary and unlikely. But I think it's a reasonable simplification. The same is true of holding the dividend yields constant over the four years.

I didn't show the effect of rebalancing the diversified portfolio in the sequence of returns examples above. So, here it is.

Annual rebalancing using the Year Four crash example is shown below.

- Starting Allocations

45% PEY = $100,000 * 0.45 = $45,000

30% BND = $100,000 * 0.30 = $30,000

10% RING = $100,000 * 0.10 = $10,000

15% BSV = $100,000 * 0.15 = $15,000

- Year One Ending Position Values

PEY – Year One Ending Position Value (+8%), $45,000 * 1.08 = $48,600

BND – Year One Ending Position Value (+0%), $30,000 * 1.00 = $30,000

RING – Year One Ending Position Value (+0%), $10,000 * 1.00 = $10,000

BSV – Year One Ending Position Value (+0%), $15,000 * 1.00 = $15,000

Year One Ending Portfolio Value = $103,600 ($48,600 + $30,000 + $10,000 + $15,000)

- Rebalanced Positions at the Start of Year Two

45% PEY = $103,600 * 0.45 = $46,620

30% BND = $103,600 * 0.30 = $31,080

10% RING = $103,600 * 0.10 = $10,360

15% BSV = $103,600 * 0.15 = $15,540

- Year Two Ending Position Values

PEY - Year Two Ending Position Value (+8%), $46,620 * 1.08 = $50,350

BND - Year Two Ending Position Value (+0%), $31,080 * 1.00 = $31,080

RING - Year Two Ending Position Value (+0%), $10,360 * 1.00 = $10,360

BSV - Year Ending Position Value (+0%), $15,540 * 1.00 = $15,540

Year Two Ending Portfolio Value = $107,330 ($50,350 + $31,080 + $10,360 + $15,540)

- Rebalanced Positions at the Start of Year Three

45% PEY = $107,330 * 0.45 = $48,298

30% BND = $107,330 * 0.30 = $32,199

10% RING = $107,330 * 0.10 = $10,733

15% BSV = $107,330 * 0.15 = $16,099

- Year Three Ending Portfolio Value = $111,193 ($52,162 + $32,199 + $10,733 + $16,099)

PEY - Year Three Ending Position Value (+8%), $48,298 * 1.08 = $52,162

BND - Year Three Ending Position Value (+0%), $32,199 * 1.00 = $32,199

RING - Year Three Ending Position Value (+0%), $10,733 * 1.00 = $10,733

BSV - Year Three Ending Position Value (+0%), $16,099 * 1.00 = $16,099

- Rebalanced Positions at the Start of Year Four

45% PEY = $111,193 * 0.45 = $50,037

30% BND = $111,193 * 0.30 = $33,358

10% RING = $111,193 * 0.10 = $11,119

15% BSV = $111,193 * 0.15 = $16,679

- Year Four Ending Portfolio Value = $100,319 ($52,162 + $32,199 + $10,733 + $16,099)

PEY - Year Four Ending Position Value (-30%), $52,162 * 0.70 = $36,513

BND - Year Four Ending Position Value (+10%), $32,199 * 1.10 = $35,419

RING - Year Four Ending Position Value (+10%), $10,733 * 1.10 = $11,806

BSV - Year Four Ending Position Value (+3%), $16,099 * 1.03 = $16,581

The portfolio value of $100,319 at the end of Year Four after annual rebalancing is slightly higher than the original starting balance. Your Forever Retirement is intact.

The effects of the Year One crash example with annual rebalancing are added below.

- Starting Allocations

45% PEY = $100,000 * 0.45 = $45,000

30% BND = $100,000 * 0.30 = $30,000

10% RING = $100,000 * 0.10 = $10,000

15% BSV = $100,000 * 0.15 = $15,000

- Year One Market Value Changes

PEY - Year One Ending Position Value (-30%), $45,000 * 0.70 = $31,500

BND - Year One Ending Position Value (+10%), $30,000 * 1.10 = $33,000

RING - Year One Ending Position Value (+10%), $10,000 * 1.10 = $11,000

BSV - Year One Ending Position Value (+3%), $15,000 * 1.03 = $15,450

Year One Ending Portfolio Value = $90,950 ($31,500 + $33,000 + $11,000 + $15,450)

- Rebalanced Positions at the Start of Year Two

45% PEY = $90,950 * 0.45 = $40,928

30% BND = $90,950 * 0.30 = $27,285

10% RING = $90,950 * 0.10 = $9,095

15% BSV = $90,950 * 0.15 = $13,643

- Year Two Market Value Changes

PEY - Year Two Ending Position Value (+8%), $40,928 * 1.08 = $44,202

BND - Year Two Ending Position Value (+0%), $27,285 * 1.00 = $27,285

RING - Year Two Ending Position Value (+0%), $9,095 * 1.00 = $9,095

BSV - Year Two Ending Position Value (+0%), $13,643 * 1.00 = $13,643

Year Two Ending Portfolio Value = $94,225 ($44,202 + $27,285 + $9,095 + $13,643)

- Rebalanced Positions at the Start of Year Three

45% PEY = $94,225 * 0.45 = $42,401

30% BND = $94,225 * 0.30 = $28,268

10% RING = $94,225 * 0.10 = $9,423

15% BSV = $94,225 * 0.15 = $14,134

- Year Three Market Value Changes

PEY - Year Three Ending Position Value (+8%), $42,401 * 1.08 = $45,793

BND - Year Three Ending Position Value (+0%), $28,268 * 1.00 = $28,268

RING - Year Three Ending Position Value (+0%), $9,423 * 1.00 = $9,423

BSV - Year Three Ending Position Value (+0%), $14,134 * 1.00 = $14,134

Year Three Ending Portfolio Value = $97,618 ($45,793 + $28,268 + $9,423 + $14,134)

- Rebalanced Positions at the Start of Year Four

45% PEY = $97,618 * 0.45 = $43,928

30% BND = $97,618 * 0.30 = $29,285

10% RING = $97,618 * 0.10 = $9,761

15% BSV = $97,618 * 0.15 = $14,643

- Year Four Market Value Changes

PEY - Year Four Ending Position Value (+8%), $43,928 * 1.08 = $45,793

BND - Year Four Ending Position Value (+0%), $29,285 * 1.00 = $29,285

RING - Year Four Ending Position Value (+0%), $9,761 * 1.00 = $9,761

BSV - Year Four Ending Position Value (+0%), $14,643 * 1.00 = $14,643

Year Four Ending Position Value = $99,482 ($45,793 + $29,285 + $9,761 + $14,643)

$99,482 is slightly ahead of the non-rebalanced result of $99,131. And the overall loss is too small to threaten your Forever Retirement.

Withdrawal Strategy Takeaways

After thinking through the results of various ways of drawing supplemental income from your retirement Nest Egg you can see some clear tradeoffs.

- Tradeoffs

1. The higher your annual withdrawal rate the more likely you'll run out of money.
2. The longer you live the more likely you'll run out of money.
3. The lower your withdrawal rate the more money you need in your Nest Egg when you retire.
4. The more your money is concentrated in one asset class the more exposed you are to a market crash in that asset – especially if the crash happens early in your retirement.

- Other Takeaways

1. A properly diversified portfolio makes a crash less painful.
2. Rebalancing improves overall returns.
3. Using your Average Dividend Rate as your Withdrawal Rate allows your money to potentially last forever.
4. A withdrawal rate higher than 4% greatly increases the probability you'll run out of money.

- Forever Retirement Takeaways

1. Allocate your retirement Nest Egg at least among the four Permanent Portfolio asset classes. Additional asset classes are okay if they are sufficiently uncorrelated. If you want to use asset class subcategories, like US Stocks and Foreign Stocks

or US Treasury Bonds and **Corporate Bonds**, count the subcategories as part of the overall category (i.e. US Treasury Bonds and Corporate Bonds together make your allocation to Bonds).

2. Choose dividend paying securities to represent your asset classes as much as possible.
3. Make your withdrawal rate less than 4% per year. The closer to your Average Dividend Rate the better.
4. Set up a rebalancing rule for your portfolio. Once a year isn't bad.

Protection from Adverse Regulations and Laws

You heard about this in the section on Risks from Acts of Congress.

I'll elaborate.

A strategy combining the elements listed below provides some protection from adverse changes in regulations and laws.

1. Pay attention. Identify threats coming from changing political winds early. Give yourself time to get out of their way.
2. As much as possible, invest in "liquid" assets. This reduces the amount of time you need to "get out of the way".
3. Spread your money over multiple legal categories. Possibilities include a Roth IRA, a Traditional IRA, a non-tax-deferred brokerage account, real estate, annuities, life insurance, precious metals (coins or bullion), fine art, bank accounts, and cash. Diversification limits your losses in case you can't get out of the way fast enough.
4. Use multiple financial institutions and multiple kinds of financial institutions. For example, Banks, Mutual Fund Companies, Brokerages, Insurance Companies, Investment

Management Companies. This is another way to diversify and limit your losses.

5. Keep assets in more than one country. Yet another way to diversify.

6. Set up ways to quickly transfer money from one institution and country to another with a minimum of fuss. Like investing in **liquid assets**, creating transfer mechanisms in advance reduces the amount of time you need to get out of the way. The transfers will take less time, and you will already know how to make them.

The more of these elements you implement in your strategy, the safer your forever retirement will be from changes in regulations and laws.

Allow for Future Lifestyle Improvements

Allowing for future improvements in your lifestyle is simple. Generate increases in income faster than the inflation rate.

There are a number of ways to generate more income.

You could work part-time or start a business.

You could, periodically, purchase an immediate annuity with a small portion of your Nest Egg. Depending on your age and prevailing interest rates, the annuity could provide monthly income for the rest of your life. It could do it safely, and at a higher payout rate than would be prudent if your Nest Egg withdrawal rate was that high.

The annuity, for example, might payout from 5% to 8% of the premium (the purchase price of the annuity).

I've considered buying a small annuity contract every couple of years using only the growth in our Nest Egg to fund the purchases. Right now, that's not part of our Income Plan. But, it's still an option for future consideration.

You could draw more income from your Nest Egg by increasing your withdrawal rate. Increasing your withdrawal rate, however, is the way to go broke slowly, then suddenly.

Or, you could grow your Nest Egg faster than the Base Rate (your withdrawal rate plus the inflation rate).

The inflation rate is beyond your control. Although, you can defend yourself from inflation using the methods described in the sections on Inflation and Hyperinflation.

Market growth rates are equally beyond your control. Stocks go up over the long-term. But they fluctuate wildly along the way. All markets go up and down.

The best you can do is invest in a broadly uncorrelated portfolio of asset classes that pay dividends.

Asset class selection, allocation percentages, security selection, and your withdrawal rate are the variables you directly control.

To increase the probability your portfolio will grow faster than the Base Rate your Withdrawal Rate should be as low as possible.

If the markets carry your portfolio upwards at a 7% annual rate, inflation is 3% per year and your Withdrawal Rate is 4% your growth above the Base Rate is zero (7% -3% -4% = 0%).

If, under the same conditions, your Withdrawal Rate is 5% you consume your capital (you go broke slowly). Your portfolio isn't keeping up with inflation (7% -3% -5% = -1%). Even though the dollar denominated value of your Nest Egg increases, its purchasing power declines.

On the other hand, if your Withdrawal Rate is 3%, you grow your portfolio faster than the Base Rate by 1% per year (7% -3% -3% = 1%).

Eventually, maintaining your 3% Withdrawal Rate, you'll improve your lifestyle without threatening your Forever Retirement.

ELEVEN

Managing Withdrawals

O bviously, you control exactly how much you withdraw from your retirement accounts.

You control exactly when you make the withdrawals.

After reading the previous section, you have a pretty good idea of how to implement these choices.

The real question is can you control yourself.

Can You Control Yourself?

What will you do when you feel you need more money? Will you stick to your withdrawal plan? Or, will you give in to the urge to splurge?

Will you be able to control how much you withdraw and when?

Your felt need for income will drive these decisions.

Your felt need comes from your lifestyle, monthly spending, emergencies, temptations, and the amount of income available from sources other than your Nest Egg.

To improve your self-control, plan for emergencies and reduce temptations.

If you don't have a Retirement Spending Plan (a budget) either actual or projected, you should create one. Make it a priority.

You don't have to budget every month. But you should have a pretty good idea of what your average spending is, or will be.

Your plan should specify where the money will come from to cover emergencies. And you know there will be emergencies.

Your "Emergency Fund" is just as important in retirement as in all other phases of life.

Reduce temptations by including a budget allocation to a special spending saving account. This is sort of "Mad Money". If your Mad Money account has enough in it to cover the cost of your temptation, you can splurge without remorse. If it doesn't, you can calculate how long it will take to accumulate the necessary amount.

There are many good personal finance books describing budgeting methods. My contribution is, "Paycheck to Paycheck, Crisis to Crisis".

There are many retirement planning books to help you figure out how much income you'll need. These are my books on the topic, "Are You Starting to Think About Retirement?" and "How Much Is Enough to Retire?".

Whatever method of budgeting you use, it's essential to have a realistic Spending Plan. One that covers your normal living expenses (needs and wants) and allows for the inevitable emergencies.

Here are the steps for Controlling Withdrawals.

1. Put your Spending Plan in place, including Emergency Fund saving and saving for special purchases, "Mad Money".
2. Identify and add up your sources of retirement income other than Nest Egg withdrawals.

3. Figure out how much you'll need to draw from your Nest Egg on a regular basis, probably monthly.
4. Determine if the regular withdrawals you need are sustainable. That means you have to determine if you'll be able to continue the needed rate of withdrawal forever with a high confidence level. If not, stop and reconsider your spending plan. You might have to reconsider your entire Integrated Retirement Plan.
5. If your planned Withdrawal Rate is sustainable, research the financial institutions managing your bank account and your Nest Egg. Determine the best way to fully automate your regular withdrawals.
6. Implement your fully automated withdrawal process. If possible, set up regular automatic transfers.
7. Reconsider your Spending Plan and Withdrawal Rate periodically. Probably annually.

Above all, remember your plan.

Your Spending Plan, your Income Plan, your Investing Plan, and your Withdrawal Plan are the structure of your Forever Retirement.

Keep the structure strong.

TWELVE

Develop an Integrated Retirement Plan

A n Integrated Retirement Plan starts with the answers to four questions

1. What are you going to do?
2. Where will you do it?
3. Who are you going to do it with?
4. When will you do it?

My books, "Are You Starting to Think About Retirement?" and "How to Decide What to Do When You Retire" cover these topics.

Your Spending Plan

After answering the four questions, figure out how much income you'll need.

Your Spending Plan, your projected budget, is the best tool for the job. My book, "How Much Is Enough to Retire?" can help.

· · ·

Your Income Plan

Knowing your required income, you can figure out where it'll come from.

Common income sources include:

1. Social Security (get an estimate of your Social Security benefit from www.socialsecurity.gov)
2. Employer Pension
3. Veterans Administration benefits (if you have a service-connected disability)
4. Annuities
5. Part-time employment
6. A lifestyle business
7. And, finally – Your Nest Egg (savings)

When you have good estimates of how much you'll need and how much you'll receive from your other income sources, calculate how much you'll have to draw from your Retirement Portfolio (Nest Egg).

Income Needed from Nest Egg =

Required Income – Social Security – Employer Pension – Annuity Payments – Other Income Sources

Each element of the equation will vary depending on when you will retire. You may have to make several passes (iterations) through all of the various Plans before you finally get one you like and can execute.

Your Investing Plan

You will, of course, go your own way.

You may think, as I have in the past, "I can tolerate risk better than other people. I know the market will recover. When it crashes, I'll have the courage to ride it out and not sell low."

Yes, Mr Buffett. Of course, you will.

"Russell Kinnell of Morningstar has a revealing article and chart comparing the performance of the average fund with the average investor, broken down by category like US stocks or municipal bonds. This higher-level view is useful because it takes out any noise you might get from just looking at a specific mutual fund. Did the average investor's market timing efforts pay off? Here are the results, broken down into the past 3, 5, and 10-year periods."

	Avg. 3-Yr Total Return	Ast-Wgt 3-Yr Investor Return	Avg Fund vs Avg Investor	Avg. 5-Yr Total Return	Ast-Wgt 5-Yr Investor Return	Avg Fund vs Avg Investor	Avg. 10-Yr Total Return	Ast-Wgt 10-Yr Investor Return	Avg Fund vs Avg Investor
Category									
US Stock	10.04	9.80	0.24	1.55	0.75	0.80	7.89	6.88	1.01
Sector Stock	9.29	8.28	1.02	1.54	1.07	0.47	9.44	9.07	0.37
Intl Equity	5.18	5.10	0.08	2.43	-3.01	0.58	9.95	6.84	3.11
Balanced	7.49	7.72	-0.23	2.08	2.49	-0.41	6.37	5.53	0.84
Taxable Bond	6.94	5.75	1.19	5.80	5.16	0.64	5.63	4.76	0.87
Muni Bond	5.91	4.49	1.42	4.71	3.33	1.38	4.06	2.71	1.35
All Funds	7.59	7.36	2.23	2.02	1.49	0.53	7.05	6.10	0.95

"We see that across almost every category and every timeframe, the investor return lags the fund return. That gap also tends to grow over time, with an average underperformance of nearly 1% a year over the last 10 years. That's a lot of money. The S&P 500 is basically back to it's all-time high back in 2007, even though it was a crazy roller coaster in between, and it seems most people didn't time it correctly. It would be wise to remember this consistent underperformance the next time you think about market timing, or buying something simply because it did well in the recent past."

"Market Timing Is Hard: Actual Investor Returns Lag Fund Returns"

https://www.mymoneyblog.com/nvestor-returns-vs-fund-returns.html

. . .

<u>You Need a System</u>

The rest of us need fortification. We need a system that:

1. Reduces our losses on the way down.
2. Signals us to "do" something active and constructive on the way down.
3. Doesn't depend on forecasting (guessing) when or which way the market will go next.
4. Has the intellectual support of history and academic research.
5. Throws off cash (dividends) throughout the bear market.
6. Improves our gains on the way up.

In short, the rest of us need to use Asset Allocation with Rebalancing as our base system. Tweaking the security selections, the allocation percentages, and the rebalancing trigger to our individual tastes.

We can then, with a calmness of spirit, gaze in awe at "Mr Buffett's" ability to ride out the storm.

By the way, the real Warren Buffett accumulates a larger and larger cash position as the market rises to ever new highs. When it crashes, he BUYS.

Our friend, the fake Mr Buffett, is fully invested as the market rises to new highs. When the market crashes, he can't buy. He has no cash. He just watches his portfolio plummet.

Using Asset Allocation with Rebalancing, if your rebalancing trigger is a threshold amount (or %) your system signals you to behave more like the real Warren Buffett. It tells you to sell some of what is high to raise cash and to buy more of what is low.

<u>My System</u>

As you know by now, I use an Asset Allocation with Rebalancing system.

The Mutual Fund ticker symbols below represent the four basic asset classes of The Permanent Portfolio. They are the securities I use in the Asset Allocation with Rebalancing retirement account.

USSBX – Cash (Short-Term Bonds)

UGMVX – Bonds (Stable Value)

USAGX - Precious Metals (Precious Metal Miners)

USISX – Stocks (US Stocks)

USIFX – Stocks (International Stocks)

I use dynamic allocations that increase the proportion of Cash to Stocks as the **CAPE Ratio** of the S&P500 Index increases.

Today, in 2019, the CAPE Ratio is above average. This drives my current allocation percentages to:

45% - USSBX – Cash (Short-Term Bonds)

10% - UGMVX – Bonds (Stable Value)

15% - USAGX - Precious Metals (Precious Metal Miners)

15% - USISX – Stocks (US Stocks)

15% - USIFX – Stocks (International Stocks)

I use a threshold trigger set at 1.0%. The threshold trigger is the difference between the current actual value and the value calculated by my allocation formula. When the difference is greater than the threshold trigger, my system gives me a buy or sell signal.

To trigger a trade, the system requires a minimum 1.0% difference in each of at least two asset classes. One must be above its allocation and one below. Obviously, the trade is to sell some of the higher asset class and buy some of the lower one.

Often, only one asset class has a trade signal. This happens when the opposite side of the trade is split among two or more asset classes.

I might see a +1% signal for cash (indicating buy more) and at the same time see a -0.5% signal in both stocks and in precious metals (indicating sell some). In this case, I do nothing.

When another asset signals a trade in the opposite direction with at least a full 1% signal (-1% in the example), I set up an exchange from the asset above its allocation to the asset below its allocation.

The signal quantities are never exactly the same.

For example, I might get a sell signal for USSBX in the amount of $2,500. And a buy signal for USISX in the amount of $1,800. In this situation, I exchange $1,800 of USSBX for $1,800 of USISX.

Normal market fluctuations cause me to trade in this account between 3 and 7 times per month.

I know this is too complicated for most people and probably too much trading.

To slow it down and make it simpler, increase the Threshold percentage and eliminate the dynamic allocations.

If I were to do that in this account, I would set the Threshold percentage at 2.0% and use fixed allocations as shown below.

30% - USSBX – Cash (Short-Term Bonds)

5% - UGMVX – Bonds (Stable Value)

15% - USAGX - Precious Metals (Precious Metal Miners)

25% - USISX – Stocks (US Stocks)

25% - USIFX – Stocks (International Stocks)

My fixed allocation choices are not a recommendation. They're pretty arbitrary. And, as I said earlier, tweaking them doesn't make much difference in the overall performance of the portfolio.

Your Withdrawal Plan

I argued earlier you should withdraw less than 4% of your Nest Egg per year.

The 4% Rule assumes you start with an amount equal to 4% and you increase the amount with inflation every year regardless of the resulting withdrawal rate.

After the first year, the withdrawal rate will vary depending on the inflation rate and where the market goes.

Rigidly following the 4% Rule increases the Sequence of Returns risks significantly.

To protect your forever retirement, I recommend using a starting withdrawal rate below 4% and as close to your actual Dividend Rate as possible.

Even better would be to hold your withdrawal rate constant. If you start with 3%, continue withdrawing no more than 3%. As your Nest Egg grows, the amount of money your 3% gets you will increase too.

If the growing amount provides more than you need, well that's a pretty good problem.

If it doesn't, you can tighten your budget a bit, or increase your withdrawal rate as little as possible. Maybe both.

There's an obvious problem. What do you do when the market falls and simple arithmetic increases your withdrawal rate even though you're withdrawing the same amount of money?

If your withdrawal rate was initially set at the dividend rate, you simply don't need to worry about it. Just continue taking the same amount of money and know that your dividends, even if they are reduced, will cover most of your withdrawals. The market recovery will take care of the rest.

If your initial withdrawal rate is much higher than your dividend rate, the risk to your Forever Retirement is increased.

If possible, tighten your budget until the recovery is apparent. Avoid adding cost of living (inflation) adjustments to your withdrawals.

Here is my view of the relative safety of various Withdrawal Rate responses to a crash in order from most safe to least safe.

1. The safest response is to adjust your withdrawal rate so that is no higher than the new, post-crash, dividend rate.
2. Next safest is to reduce your withdrawals to maintain a constant withdrawal rate.
3. Less safe is to maintain a constant withdrawal amount, allowing your withdrawal rate to increase as the market falls.
4. Least safe is to increase the size of your withdrawals by adding inflation or lifestyle adjustments. This could lead to going broke slowly, then suddenly.

My Withdrawal Plan

I'm pulling the trigger on my retirement in a couple of months. Probably only weeks after this book is published.

My income plan includes my Social Security, my wife's Social Security, and a small pension from a previous employer.

We paid off our mortgage several years ago and we live pretty frugally. Consequently, these three income sources cover 80% of our retirement budget.

Instead of taking monthly distributions from our "**qualified retirement accounts**", we've accumulated some money in taxable accounts.

The taxable accounts are invested in dividend-paying securities and the dividend payments from these accounts are enough to close our 20% income gap.

Our "tax-advantaged" retirement accounts (Nest Egg) will continue growing without interruption except for the annual **RMD** (Required Minimum Distribution) withdrawals forced on us by the IRS (Internal Revenue Service).

The money from RMDs will be added to our taxable accounts and invested in dividend-paying securities. This will increase our dividend income over time.

Most likely, this process will keep our monthly income increasing faster than inflation.

If inflation eventually overtakes our income and withdrawal plans, we'll be able to supplement our income by taking withdrawals from our Roth IRA accounts.

Roth IRAs are not subject to the RMD requirement. They'll continue to grow tax-free until we need them.

What You Need to Do

What you need to do, in general terms, is simple.

Your Integrated Retirement Plan starts with knowing what you're going to do during your retirement. What it will be about – your purpose.

With that knowledge, calculate how much income you need to support what you're going to do.

Then figure out how much income you'll have from sources like Social Security, Pensions, and Annuities.

The difference between what you need and the sum of your non-Nest Egg sources is your Income Gap.

Fill your Income Gap with a combination of withdrawals from your Nest Egg and by earning new money from work or from a business.

Keep your Nest Egg withdrawals below 4% of the value of your portfolio.

Keep yourself in good health and physically fit.

And, enjoy your Forever Retirement.

THIRTEEN

Develop a Process

Developing a process means getting into the weeds. Get dirty digging for details.

The first details you need are the answers to the four questions.

1. What are you going to do?
2. Where will you do it?
3. Who are you going to do it with?
4. When will you do it?

Do you know what you're going to do, where, when, and with whom? If not, read "Are You Starting to Think About Retirement?" and "How to Decide What to Do When You Retire". Then get started figuring it out.

When you have those answers, then get into the weeds of your Spending Plan, your Income Plan, your Investing Plan, and your Withdrawal Plan.

Do you know how much income you'll need? My book, "How Much Is

Enough to Retire?", will help you figure it out. But you have to do the work.

Do you know how much you can expect from Social Security, Pensions, Annuities, or other sources of regular retirement income?

www.socialsecurity.gov will estimate your benefits for any proposed retirement year. You'll have to talk to your Human Resources department to find out about employer pensions or to your insurance company about annuity payouts.

Do the math. If your Income Gap amounts to 4% or more of your projected Nest Egg you need to revise your plan.

Perhaps you can delay retirement to build up the Nest Egg and allow your Social Security benefit to continue to increase 8% per year.

Maybe you could partially retire. Work part-time and delay making withdrawals from your Nest Egg while you allow it to grow.

The key is to do the work.

Get the detail.

Figure it out.

Make a plan.

FOURTEEN

Execute

_____

W hen you have a plan that works. One that supports what you want to do and is sustainable forever, then just do it.

Execute.

FIFTEEN

Summary and Conclusions

There is a real chance – a non-zero probability – you will live longer than you think. Maybe much longer.

This possibility implies several things.

1. Your retirement savings might need to last much longer than your current planning horizon.
2. You probably need to start your retirement with a bigger Nest Egg than you thought.
3. Purpose, meaning, and health are going to be even more important than you expected.

Do some research. See for yourself if I'm right.

Answer the Four Questions and create your own Integrated Retirement Plan.

You're going to need it.

SIXTEEN

Definitions

Allocation = The amount of your Nest Egg invested in a particular asset class or the various amounts invested in all selected asset classes. This is usually expressed as a percentage of the current value of the portfolio (Nest Egg).

Annuity = *"An annuity is a financial product that pays out a fixed stream of payments to an individual. These financial products are primarily used as an income stream for retirees. Annuities are created and sold by financial institutions, which accept and invest funds from individuals. Upon annuitization, the holding institution will issue a stream of payments at a later point in time."*

From https://www.investopedia.com/terms/a/annuity.asp, 2019

Asset = An asset is a thing of value. In the context of investments, it's an object of investment that is expected to retain or increase in value over time. Examples are the value of the home you own, your 401k, the sum of all of your bank accounts, and the cash value of your life insurance.

Asset Class = An asset class is a category of assets sharing similar characteristics. Some examples of asset classes are stocks, bonds, commodities, precious metals, real estate, and collectables.

Balance = The current value of an investment account or position including principle and returns.

Balanced Fund = A mutual fund or ETF that includes a diversified portfolio of asset classes, usually a combination of stocks and bonds. The balanced fund regularly rebalances its portfolio. Target Date Funds are representative of balanced funds.

CAPE Ratio (Cyclically Adjusted Price-to-Earnings ratio) = *"The CAPE ratio is a valuation measure that uses real earnings per share (EPS) over a 10-year period to smooth out fluctuations in corporate profits that occur over different periods of a business cycle. The CAPE ratio, using the acronym for cyclically adjusted price-to-earnings ratio, was popularized by Yale University professor Robert Shiller. It is also known as the Shiller P/E ratio. The ratio is generally applied to broad equity indices to assess whether the market is undervalued or overvalued."*

https://www.investopedia.com/terms/c/cape-ratio.asp

Collectables = Any non-traditional financial asset for which there's an existing market. Examples include fine art (paintings, sculpture, etc), rare coins, rare postage stamps, baseball cards, and comic books. The process of buying and selling collectables is more difficult than with traditional financial assets. And, the spread between the price at which you can sell an item and the price at which you could buy the same item is generally larger.

Commodities = Common basic goods best represented by agricultural products like wheat, corn, or coffee, and by minerals extracted from the earth like iron, copper, or manganese. Commodities are traded on exchanges in the form of futures contracts. A futures contract is a promise to deliver a certain amount of a specific commodity on a specific date in the future. Producers of commodity goods sell futures contracts in order to lock in a price for their products well in advance of production. This allows the producer to ensure a profit even if the price of the commodity suffers a large decline during the intervening production cycle.

Consumer Price Index (CPI) = *"The Consumer Price Index (CPI) is a measure of the average change over time in the prices paid by urban consumers for a market basket of consumer goods and services. Indexes are available for the U.S. and various geographic areas. Average price data for select utility, automotive fuel, and food items are also available."*

From the Bureau of Labor Statistics website https://www.bls.gov/cpi/

Corporate Bonds = Debt contracts issued by a corporation. The corporation promises to periodically pay a specific amount of money in interest to the holder of the contract (bond) until a specific "maturity" date. The corporation further promises to deliver to the bond holder a specific amount of money on the maturity date. All this is in exchange for the initial purchase price of the bond. After the initial sale of a corporate bond, they can be traded on exchanges in a manner similar to the trading of corporate stocks. Although the market prices of the traded bonds vary, the holder of the bond at the end of the borrowing period (the maturity date) receives the amount promised by the corporation in the contract (bond).

Cost of Living Adjustments (COLA) = An automatic increase in payments tied to the recent inflation rate, usually the CPI.

Diversifying = Spreading your wealth (normally investments in securities) among various asset types to reduce the risk your wealth will be destroyed by the collapse of a single asset.

Dividend Yield = The value of dividends paid per year by a stock divided by the stock's current price. The dividend yield goes up when the dividend payout increases. It also goes up if the price of the stock falls and the dividend payout stays the same.

Drawdown = The decrease in the value of an investment. Usually by a significant amount and for a significant length of time.

EFT (Exchange Traded Fund) = An exchange traded fund is a security made up of a bundle of other securities in accordance with a stated investment strategy. Shares of EFT's are traded on public exchanges just like stocks.

Exchange (as a noun) = A public exchange is a place, either physical or virtual, that matches willing buyers with willing sellers of a particular class of goods and facilitates the trade.

. . .

Exchange (as a verb) = In this book, exchange means to move a specific amount of value denominated in currency, from one mutual fund to another in a single transaction. Exchanges are normally allowed between funds within a single family. That is, funds owned and managed by the same company. Exchanges are performed within the Mutual Fund Company platform. They are not permitted on third-party platforms or public exchanges.

Expected Return = Your expectation of the growth in the value of your principle investment plus the dividends and interest you expect to receive over a specific period of time. It may be expressed as an annual percentage.

Exposure (or Exposed) = Having some portion of your money (Nest Egg) invested in the asset class or security to which you are "exposed".

Index Fund = An ETF or Mutual Fund that intentionally tries to track the performance of an established stock or other published index. The Dow Jones Industrial Average and the S&P 500 are examples of published indexes tracked by index funds.

Institutional Investors = Organizations that invest large sums of money for the purpose of generating long-term returns for some specific purpose. Examples are pension funds, university endowments, philanthropic foundations, and hedge funds.

Liabilities = Debts; anything you owe to another. In the context of finance, it is normally the sum of all the money you have borrowed plus the accumulated interest owed. Examples are your mortgage, your credit card balances, and your student loan debt. Also, the possibility of incurring debt from a court judgement.

Liquid Assets = Assets that can be quickly and reliably converted into cash or other asset classes, even if at a loss.

Long-Term = As used in this book - a subjective opinion about how much time must pass before the risk of inflation is likely to be greater than the risk of a drawdown to the purchasing power of your Nest Egg.

Mutual Fund = A financial vehicle made up of a pool of money from the investing public. The fund uses that money to buy other securities, usually stocks and bonds. The mutual fund's value is the sum of the values of the securities it buys. Its value is known as the Net Asset Value or NAV. Mutual Funds trade on the private platforms of the mutual fund management companies. They also trade on the public exchanges, but not during normal exchange trading hours. Trades are set up during normal hours and executed after the exchanges close. Trades execute at a price equal to the fund NAV calculated using the closing prices of underlying securities at the end of the trading day.

Nest Egg = The money you've saved and invested to provide income throughout your retirement

Net Worth = The sum of all of your assets less the sum of all of your liabilities.

Portfolio = The various securities, taken as a group, that make up your Nest Egg investments.

. . .

Position = An actual investment of any amount in a specific security.

Precious Metals = A subset of commodities, precious metals are commonly and historically used as jewelry and money. Gold and silver are the most prominent examples. Platinum and palladium are also in the category. There are many ways to trade precious metals, especially gold and silver. You can buy and sell the physical metal in the form of coins or bullion bars. Futures contracts are available just like other commodities. ETF's (Exchange Traded Funds) and Trusts that represent a specific quantity of metal held by a third-party trade on stock exchanges. The shares of mining companies producing precious metals also trade on stock exchanges.

Principle = The original amount of money used to create an investment account or position. It does not include the returns.

Qualified Retirement Account = A savings or investing account packaged in a legal construct authorized by law for the purpose of encouraging people to save for their own retirement. Accounts of this kind include Traditional IRAs (Individual Retirement Account), Roth IRAs, Employer-Based 401k's, 403b's, and others. Each kind has its own restrictions and benefits. They share the general feature of reducing the amount of taxes owed on the money in the accounts.

Real Estate = Ownership of land or buildings that occupy physical space. You can, of course, have title to a specific piece of real estate. Beyond that, funds and trusts exist that trade on stock exchanges. These funds and trusts generally represent partial ownership of a portfolio of many parcels of real estate. Companies whose primary business is real estate development or management are also traded on stock exchanges as common stocks.

Rebalance = Action to buy and sell specific amounts of the asset classes that make up the portfolio (Nest Egg) in order to restore the portfolio to the desired asset allocations. Generally, this requires selling a portion of the asset classes that recently increased in value and buying more of the asset classes that recently decreased in value.

Returns = The total increase in the value of your investment or Nest Egg over a period of time. Usually expressed as a percentage of the initial value at the beginning of the time period. The components of return are (1) the money produced by the investment (interest, dividends, or distributed profits) plus (2) the increase in the market value of the asset (what you can sell it for now compared to what you paid for it).

Revert to the Mean = The tendency of most variables to fluctuate around a long-term average or trend line. The old saying, "What goes up must come down" is an expression of this phenomena. Although, it is equally, and importantly, true that what goes down will go up.

Risk Mitigation = Any actions that are taken to reduce the negative effects on your Nest Egg that might be caused by risks you have identified.

RMD (Required Minimum Distributions) = Required Minimum Distributions are a feature of the law authorizing Traditional IRAs and 401k's. Essentially, you are required to withdraw about 4% of your Traditional IRA or 401k every year starting in the year your age reaches 70.5 years. The withdrawal percentage increases every year. The intent of the law is for the IRS to recover taxes on the previously untaxed money in these accounts before you die.

Robo Advisor = An investment platform that automatically manages your portfolio. Generally, it invests your money in a broadly diversified selection of ETF's with risk-optimized allocation percentages. Rebalancing is done when position values become misaligned by more than an established threshold amount. When money is added or withdrawn from the account, the Robo Advisor also takes those opportunities to rebalance.

Safe Withdrawal Rate = The amount expressed as a percentage, you can withdraw from your Nest Egg without fear of running out of money during your lifetime(s). In reality, this is an imaginary concept. There is no such thing as perfect safety. We must be satisfied with a high probability of success (a low probability of running out of money).

Securities = the investment products you can actually buy and sell on public exchanges. Stocks, Bonds, Mutual Funds, ETF's (exchange traded funds), and Futures Contracts are examples of securities.

Solvent = Having a positive net worth. That is, the sum of your assets is greater than or equal to the sum of your liabilities.

Sovereign Bonds = Debt contracts issued by nation-states. Sovereign Bonds are usually perceived as less risky than corporate bonds because nation-states are less prone to bankruptcy or default. Otherwise, these debt contracts function exactly like corporate bonds.

. . .

Stocks = Fractional shares in the ownership of a company. Generally, the shares are traded on an **exchange** system in a public way. The exchange provides visibility of the changing prices of the stocks and connects willing buyers with willing sellers.

Target Date Fund = A balanced mutual fund that changes its asset allocation percentages depending on how far a certain date is in the future, the Target Date. The closer the Target Date is, the higher the percentage of bonds and the lower the percentage of stocks are held in the fund.

Tax-Advantaged Accounts = Any financial account that legally shields some or all of the **principle** or gains from taxation. Qualified Retirement Accounts are tax-advantaged. So are deferred annuities and cash-value life insurance.

The 4% Rule = The most commonly discussed withdrawal strategy. Using statistical analyses, back tested against all possible combinations of thirty-years of historical United States stock market results, use of the 4% Rule is predicted to enable your Nest Egg to last for thirty-years without running out of money with a 95% probability. A good article on The 4% Rule can be found at this link.

Ticker Symbol (Ticker) = The abbreviation, usually one to five letters, by which a security is known on a public exchange. For example, Ford Motor Company is known as "F" on the New York Stock Exchange (NYSE) and Proctor and Gambol is known as "PG".

. . .

Trade (as a verb) = Buying, selling, or exchanging securities.

Trade (as a noun) = A single buy, sell, or exchange of a security.

Transaction Costs = A cost incurred as a result of buying, selling or exchanging securities. Brokerage commissions are the most common example.

Uncorrelated = For the purpose of this book, uncorrelated means that the prices of selected asset classes vary independently from one another. In other words, the price changes in the asset classes do not go in the same direction. One may go up, another down, and a third remain unchanged. The less the price changes look the same, the more uncorrelated they are. Correlated asset classes behave in the opposite manner. When they change in price, they tend to change in approximately the same direction and magnitude.

Volatile (or Volatility) = Subject to greater than average changes in price. Higher highs and lower lows over relatively short time periods compared to other kinds of investments. Technically, volatility is simply a measure of the price changes over time for any security. However, when someone says a thing is "volatile" they mean its price swings are greater than normal.

Withdrawal Rate = The amount you withdraw from your Nest Egg over the course of one year expressed as a percentage. Withdrawal Rate = (Sum of all Withdrawals in One Year) / (Value of the Nest Egg at the beginning of the Year) * 100.

Longevity

"The Big Five" by Sanjiv Chopra

"My Plan for Living to 156" by Dan Sullivan

"Transcend: 9 Steps to Living Well Forever" by Ray Kurzweil and Terry Grossman

"Brain Rules for Aging Well" by John Medina

"The 100-Year Life" by Lynda Grafton and Andrew Scott

"The End of Aging" by Matt Ward and Aubrey De Grey

Retirement

"How to Retire?" by Olivia Greenwell

"Retired Broke" by Randy and Jane Kirk

"End of the Retirement Age" by David Kennedy

Purpose

"The Purpose Driven Life: What on Earth Am I Here For" by Rick Warren

. . .

"12 Rules for Life: An Antidote to Chaos", by Jordan B. Peterson

"Meditations", by Marcus Aurelius

"Ego Is the Enemy", by Ryan Holiday

"Life Planning for You: How to Design & Deliver the Life of Your Dreams" by George Kinder and Mary Rowland

EIGHTEEN

Reviews

D ear Reader,

If you found this book useful, please help others find it too. Leave a review of "Your Forever Retirement" at your favorite online bookstore.

Thanks,

Mel Clark

About the Author

Mel Clark writes about personal finance, retirement planning, and martial arts.

His blue-collar parents raised him and his two sisters in a wonderful environment for children.

The family, however, was always in debt, always making payments, and never saving.

As a result, Mel is compelled to share hard-won money lessons with working folks. He wants them to know the benefits of saving and investing.

You don't have to be rich to become financially independent.

Mel and his lovely wife Linda live near Virginia's Blue Ridge Parkway. They enjoy ballroom dancing, the occasional camping trip and a silly game called Bananagrams.

Mel is a graduate of the United States Military Academy at West Point and the Darden School of Business at the University of Virginia.

You can email him at clearthinkingaboutmoney@gmail.com. Your information will not be shared with anyone else.

Link to Other Books by Mel Clark

https://books2read.com/ap/xXk1N8/Mel-Clark